SELF TEACHING MANUAL
for the text
Economic Evaluation and Investment Decision Methods

Second Edition

FRANKLIN J. STERMOLE
PROFESSOR EMERITUS, COLORADO SCHOOL OF MINES
PRESIDENT, INVESTMENT EVALUATIONS CORPORATION

JOHN M. STERMOLE
ADJUNCT PROFESSOR, COLORADO SCHOOL OF MINES
VICE PRESIDENT, INVESTMENT EVALUATIONS CORPORATION

INVESTMENT EVALUATIONS CORPORATION
2000 Goldenvue Drive
Golden, Colorado 80401

Franklin J. Stermole, B.S., M.S., Ph.D., Chemical Engineering, Iowa State University, is Professor Emeritus of Mineral Economics and Chemical and Petroleum Refining Engineering at Colorado School of Mines, where he has taught since 1963, and serves as President of Investment Evaluations Corporation. He has taught economic evaluation techniques for 28 years to undergraduate and graduate students and has done economic evaluation consulting for numerous mineral and non-mineral companies. Since 1970, Frank has taught more than 500 "Economic Evaluation" short courses to over 14,000 persons from mineral and non-mineral industry companies and government agencies. In addition to the United States, the course has been presented in Australia, Canada, Colombia, France, Germany, Great Britain, Guyana, Indonesia, Mexico, Norway, Saudi Arabia, South Africa, Trinidad, and Venezuela for industry and government organizations. This domestic and foreign industrial consulting and teaching experience has had a direct effect on the applications-oriented content and organization of the text.

John M. Stermole, B.S.B.A., Finance, University of Denver, and M.S., Mineral Economics, Colorado School of Mines, is Vice-President of Investment Evaluations Corporation. In addition, since 1988, John has taught as an Adjunct Professor at Colorado School of Mines for the Departments of Mineral Economics, Chemical and Petroleum Refining Engineering and Environmental Sciences. Over the past six years, John has taught more than 75 "Economic Evaluation" short courses for mineral, petroleum and non -mineral companies and government agencies. In addition to the United States, John has presented the course in Canada, Columbia and Indonesia. Other areas of interest have included work in development of personal computer software to apply the concepts addressed throughout the textbook along with economic evaluation consulting to the resource industries. Prior to joining Investment Evaluations Corporation on a full-time basis, John gained three years of industry experience with Lowdermilk Construction of Englewood, Colorado, applying economic evaluation techniques to heavy construction projects related to mine site and development and highway construction and in replacement analyses.

Second Edition Copyright © 1993 by Investment Evaluations Corporation 2000 Goldenvue Drive, Golden, CO 80401
Ph: (303) 278-3464

Copyright © 1990 by Investment Evaluations Corporation

ISBN 1-878740-05-9
Library of Congress Catalog Card Number 92-75479

Printed in U.S.A.

TABLE OF CONTENTS

PREFACE

All of the material and concepts presented in this manual are covered in a paraphrased manner in Chapters 1 through 4 of the text, "Economic Evaluation and Investment Decision Methods", 8th Edition, 1993, by Stermole and Stermole. This material will be addressed during the first day and a half of the "Economic Evaluation" courses taught by Frank or John Stermole. Your review of the contents of this Self Teaching Manual prior to attending one of the courses will either introduce you to, or provide refresher review for general discounted cash flow criteria and concepts. Our hope with this material is that it will provide you with an initial understanding of the concepts and a more meaningful course experience.

To assist with your verification of the time value of money calculations in various case study illustrations, discrete compound interest factor tables are given at the end of this manual. The 6% discrete interest rate factor table is integrated into the manual material on page 26.

HOW TO STUDY THIS COURSE

This programmed instruction course is divided into short instructional steps called frames, which are to be studied in sequence. Most frames have two parts. The first part usually gives information and then asks a question or requires you to take some action; the second part gives the correct solution to the question.

As you study each frame, use a card or sheet of paper to conceal the correct answers until you have worked out the answers yourself. Then move the card down to reveal the printed answer. Do not look at the answer to the frame until you have made an effort to arrive at it. If you are unsure of the correct answer, study the frame again.

After each frame, in the center of the page, are three gray bars. These are the stopping places for your card. As you move the card down you will reveal the answer to the previous frame as well as the next frame.

You may write the answers or formulate them mentally, as you prefer. Some frames will require you to use pencil and paper to solve problems or work out exercises. For these frames it is best to use scratch paper.

Do not look ahead at the answers before you have made an honest effort to arrive at the correct one. You might deceive yourself by thinking that the given answer is the one you would have arrived at. Experience with this type of self-study shows this will not produce learning.

Toward the beginning of some modules are "skip ahead" frames which offer you the opportunity to by-pass certain material if you feel you already know it. If you cannot correctly solve the problems and exercises to which you skip, you should go back and study the by-passed frames.

The amount of time you spend in any one study session is just what you feel like spending. One of the benefits of programmed instruction is that you can study at your own pace for as long as you wish. However, it is best not to let too much time go by before resuming study.

The reference textbook for this Self-Teaching Manual is "Economic Evaluation and Investment Decision Methods", 8th Edition, 1993, by Stermole and Stermole. It is published by Investment Evaluations Corporation, 2000 Goldenvue Drive, Golden, CO 80401.

MODULE 1

Cash Flow Concepts

SKIP OPTION

If you are already familiar with the concepts of cash flow and arithmetic signs that cash flow components carry in economic evaluation equations you may skip to Frame 9.

1. A business normally relies on providing a service or goods to consumers. In the operation of the business it is necessary both to spend money and to earn money. Thus, money flows into the business as revenue is earned and flows out as operating expenses are paid. This inward and outward movement of money is called cash flow.

   Money paid to employees as salaries (is/is not) _____ part of a company's cash flow.

   ═══════════════════════════

   is. Salaries represent an operating expense and are an outward flow of money.

2. A salesman who generates revenue by his sales and earns commissions on them causes (inward/outward/both) _____ cash flow.

   ═══════════════════════════

   both, inward on sales revenues and outward on commission costs.

1

3. Money flowing inward can come from the sale of products, interest earned on investments, from dividends and other sources. Money flowing outward can be for salaries, leases, equipment, purchases, raw materials and other expenses. This movement of money into and out of a company's accounts is called _Cashflow_ .

─────────────────────────────

cash flow.

4. In your own words, define cash flow.

─────────────────────────────

The movement of money (funds) into and out of a company's accounts.

5. Because money spent to operate a business *subtracts* from the company's available cash, it is called *negative cash flow*. Conversely, money earned from sales, interest and dividends *adds* to the available cash and is called *positive cash flow*. As one would expect, in economic evaluations of income producing investments, expenditures are given (negative/positive) _____ signs and all income amounts are given (negative/positive) _____ signs.

─────────────────────────────

negative
positive

6. Positive cash flow moves _money in_ a company's accounts. Negative cash flow moves _money out_ a company's accounts.

─────────────────────────────

money into
money out of

7. Earned money is (+/-) _____ cash flow and moves money _into_ a company's accounts. Operating expenses are (+/-) _____ cash flow and moves money _out of_ a company's accounts.

=====================================

+, into
-, out of

8. In your own words, define negative and positive cash flow.

=====================================

Negative cash flow is money (funds) flowing outward from company accounts to pay for capital or operating expenses. For income producing economic evaluations, it carries a minus sign. Positive cash flow is money (funds) from revenues or other sources flowing into a company's accounts. In economic evaluations of income producing properties it carries a positive sign.

9. We have seen that cash flow can involve different types of expenses and different sources of income. Here are the principal components of cash flow for most income producing projects.

A. Capital Expenditures
B. Operating Costs
C. Working Capital
D. Revenue or Savings
E. Taxes

=====================================

No Response Required.

SKIP OPTION

If you are familiar with the cash flow components presented in Frame 9 and can identify the mathematical signs they carry in economic evaluation calculations for income producing properties, you may skip to Frame 16.

We will examine these cash flow components individually.

10. Capital Expenditures. This component is defined as the purchase of fixed assets, (e.g., plant and equipment) expenditure on trade investments or acquisitions of other businesses.

Because capital expenditures involve outward cash flow in economic evaluations, they carry a _____ − _____ sign.

─────────────────────

negative (or minus).

11. Operating costs are often defined as recurring expenditures over the life of a project. Examples of operating costs include labor, materials, fuel, utilities, selling expenses, administrative costs, rents, etc. This expense category carries a _____ − _____ sign.

─────────────────────

negative (minus).

12. Working capital is the money necessary to operate a business on a day-to-day basis. Such money may be utilized to meet expenditures for inventory related to raw materials, in-process materials, spare parts, cash, etc. Working Capital represents an expenditure of capital in economic evaluations and carries a _____ − _____ sign.

─────────────────────

negative (minus).

13. Revenue is income from sales, investments and dividends. It carries a _____ + _____ sign.

─────────────────────

positive.

14. Taxes include the federal and state government share of profits according to the relevant tax deductions and tax rates, and because taxes involve cash outflow, they carry a _____ − _____ sign.

═══════════════════════════════════

negative

15. You can use the acronym COWRT to help you remember these cash flow components:

    (C)apital Expenditures
    (O)perating Costs
    (W)orking Capital
    (R)evenue or Savings
    (T)axation

═══════════════════════════════════

No Response Required.

16. There are typically two distinct stages in a project: the *pre-production* stage and the *production* stage. The pre-production stage incurs the major research, exploration and development expenditures; therefore the cash flow during this stage will most typically be _____ .

═══════════════════════════════════

negative (or minus).

17. The *pre-production* stage is the investment period for the project and the cash flow for any given year of this stage will be the sum of the current operating expenditures and any capital expenditures made during that year. This sum typically represents (negative/positive) _____ cash flow.

═══════════════════════════════════

negative (or minus).

18. After production has started the project will be in the second, or *production*, stage in which money is earned. The cash flow during this period will be the revenues less current operating expenditures, capital expendi-

tures, and taxes. The net result of these values is called *"Net Cash Flow", (N.C.F.), which many people shorten to "Cash Flow" (C.F.). The terms "Cash Flow" and "Net Cash Flow"* are interchangeable.

The equation for computing Net Cash Flow is:

Net Cash Flow = Revenue - Operating Costs - Capital Costs - Taxes

The cash flow components in the above equation (are/are not) _____ correctly signed.

_____

are.

19. During which stages of a project's life are the cash flows predominantly negative? During which stages should they become positive?

_____

pre-production, production.

20. To calculate net cash flow (N.C.F.) the cash flow components must be added with attention to their respective negative and positive signs. Given revenue = $100,000, operating costs = $56,000, capital costs = $22,000 and taxes =$8,500, compute the net cash flow.

13,5 M

NCF = $100,000 - $56,000 - $22,000 - $8,500 = $13,500

21. In your own words, define Net Cash Flow.

_____

Net cash flow is the arithmetic sum of positive and negative cash flow components typically realized during a given operating period.

22. The life span of a project usually is divided into equal compounding periods which are often yearly, but may be another period such as

monthly, quarterly, or semi-annually. Cash flow must be calculated for each appropriate compounding period. As we have seen, to calculate cash flow for any time period, all expenditures during that period must be subtracted from all revenue or savings accumulated during the period. Tax is then also deducted from the remaining revenue (if any) according to the relevant formula.

Project lives are divided into equal *interest compounding periods*

interest compounding periods

23. How is cash flow calculated for a given time period?

Expenditures for the period must be subtracted from revenues or savings earned during the period.

24. To review, cash flow components for a typical project include:

1. Positive Components;

    A. Sales Revenue or Savings

2. Negative Components;

    A. Capital Costs
    B. Operating Costs
    C. Taxes

No Response Required

25. A company estimates the following cash flow components (in millions of dollars) for the next 5 years of a project:

Year	1	2	3	4	5
Total Revenue	100	150	200	300	400
Operating Costs	50	70	90	130	180
Capital Costs	60	30	20	10	
Tax		10	40	80	130
	(10)	40	50	80	90

Set up the net cash flows for the company for each of the next 5 years of this project.

═══════════════════════════

Using the definition for net cash flow (N.C.F.):
N.C.F. = Revenue - Oper. Costs - Cap. Costs - Taxes

Net Cash Flow	-10	40	50	80	90
Year	1	2	3	4	5

26. A mining company is considering the viability of sinking another shaft in an existing mine. The following cash flow components (in millions of dollars) would be realized for the next 5 years of the project's life.

Year	0	1	2	3	4
Total Revenue			45	65	100
Operating Costs	5	10	15	20	30
Capital Costs	35	50	10	5	
Taxes			2	4	10

Calculate the N.C.F.'s for the 5 years of the proposed shaft project. (-40) (-60) 18 36 60

═══════════════════════════

N.C.F.	-40	-60	18	36	60
Year	0	1	2	3	4

27. As a graphic aid to visualizing the points in a project's life at which the various cash flows occur we can draw a *Time Line Diagram* showing the start and finish of the project, with the chosen time intervals (periods) into which the project life is divided. The time line diagram also will show the cash flows for each period. Here is a time line diagram for the net cash flows solved in Frame 25:

Net Cash Flow	-10	40	50	80	90
Year	1	2	3	4	5

Another approach to time diagrams is based on using vertical lines to represent costs and revenues with costs down and revenues up.

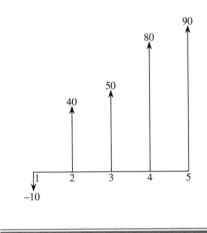

No Response Required

28. The use of time line diagrams will play an important part later in this course when we are looking at project evaluation techniques. Because of its graphic nature it provides a quick reference to the periods of a project's life and their respective cash flows.

What is the purpose of a time line diagram?

To graphically represent the cash flow for each period of a project's life.

29. Draw a time line diagram showing the net cash flows for the first five years of the example illustrated in Frame 26.

Net Cash Flow	-40	-60	18	36	60
Year	0	1	2	3	4

or

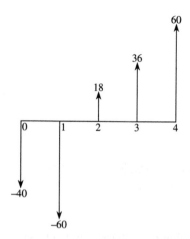

30. Project economic evaluations depend on the cash flows for the project; hence for a reliable evaluation we require detailed cash flow estimates. These aspects of accurate and careful cash flow estimating should be borne in mind:

1. Completeness – Estimates are to cover all parameters and the total period of the project.

2. Alternatives – The alternative(s) could be either implementing a new project or doing nothing. All relevant alternatives must be considered.

3. Time – Estimates of early cash flows are far more important than those for later stages of the project.

4. Taxes – Cash flows should be estimated after tax to properly evaluate the economic feasibility of a project.

You might want to use the acronym CATT to help you remember these important elements of project economic evaluations:
(C)ompleteness of estimate.
(A)lternatives that are relevant.
(T)ime importance - early cash flows are most important.
(T)axes must be included.
The acronym CATT stands for what elements in a project economic evaluation?

Completeness
Alternatives
Time
Taxes

31. You should now be sufficiently familiar with the concept of cash flow and how to calculate it, to work the following exercises:

32. Given the following two alternate projects which a company is considering, categorize and write down the cash flow components for each of the two options; calculate annual net cash flows. (All figures are expressed in millions of dollars.)

Option A: This proposal has a 4 year life and requires annual outlays for the first three years of 5, 10 and 15 in capital costs. This is expected to generate revenues of 50, 65, 80 and 100 for operating costs of 10, 11, 12 and 12, all commencing in year 1. Tax amounting to 5, 8, 10 and 12 will be paid in the respective years.

Option B: This proposal has a 6 year life and requires annual outlays for the first 5 years of 40, 20, 10, 5 and 2 in capital costs. This is expected to generate annual revenues of 10, 50, 100, 120 and 150 commencing from year 2 for operating costs of 7, 8, 10, 10, 12, and 12 starting in year 1. Tax and lease amounts of 5, 12, 15 and 18 will be paid in the final 4 yrs.

Solution to Option A:

Year	1	2	3	4
Revenue	50	65	80	100
-Oper. Costs	-10	-11	-12	-12
-Capital Costs	-5	-10	-15	0
-Taxes, Leases	-5	-8	-10	-12
Net Cash Flow	30	36	43	76

Solution to Option B:

Year	1	2	3	4	5	6
Revenue		10	50	100	120	150
-Oper. Costs	-7	-8	-10	-10	-12	-12
-Capital Costs	-40	-20	-10	-5	-2	0
-Taxes, Leases			-5	-12	-15	-18
Net Cash Flow	-47	-18	25	73	91	120

33. A mine shaft is to be sunk (or petroleum well to be drilled) in a new lease area purchased for $10 million at year 0. The capital cost expenditure breakdown over years 1 through 4 is as follows (in millions): $32, $15, $12 and $5. These capital investments will result in operating costs of $22 million beginning in year 1, which will increase by $2 million per year for each of the next four years. The annual revenue earned will be constant at $45 million per year over this period. Taxes amounting to $3, $2.5, $2.2 and $2 will be paid in the respective years beginning in year 1.

Categorize and write down cash flow components for the next four years of the company's operation and calculate annual net cash flows.

Year	0	1	2	3	4
Revenue		45.0	45.0	45.0	45.0
-Oper. Costs		-22.0	-24.0	-26.0	-28.0
-Capital Costs		-32.0	-15.0	-12.0	-5.0
-Lease	-10.0				
-Taxes		-3.0	-2.5	-2.2	-2.0
Net Cash Flow	-10.0	-12.0	3.5	4.8	10.0

34.   Cash Flow, Criterion Test:

Given the following economic proposal, categorize and write down the cash flow components. Without reference, correctly calculate the annual net cash flows. (All figures are expressed in millions)

Proposal:

A company is to expand its facilities and will require annual outlays of $110, $30, $20 and $10 on fixed assets starting years 1 through 4. This is expected to generate revenues of $100, $165, $220, $330 and $350 for operating costs of $50, $73.5, $94.5, $136.5 and $145.5 in years 1 through 5. Taxes of $5, $92 and $95 will be paid in years 3 through 5.

100	165	220	330	350
(50)	(73.5)	(94.5)	(136.5)	(145.5)
		(5)	(92)	(95)
(110)	(30)	(20)	(10)	
(60)	61.5	100.5	91.5	109.5

Cash Flow, Criterion Test Solution in Millions of Dollars:

Year	1	2	3	4	5
Revenue	100.0	165.0	220.0	330.0	350.0
-Oper. Costs	-50.0	-73.5	-94.5	-136.5	-145.5
-Capital Costs	-110.0	-30.0	-20.0	-10.0	
-Tax			-5.0	-92.0	-95.0
Net Cash Flow	-60.0	61.5	100.5	91.5	109.5

MODULE 2

Present, Future and Annual Values

SKIP OPTION

If you are familiar with the following concepts and diagrams you may skip this sequence of Frames.

A. Compound interest.
B. Interest rates.
C. Compounding formulae using "P", "F" and "A" values.
D. Compounding periods.
E. Time line diagrams for the compounding process.

1. Will $100 spent today purchase the same amount of goods and services as it would have one year ago? Probably not. The purchasing power, or worth, of money seldom is constant for a very long period of time. Last year's salary usually is a little inadequate for this years's needs. If we are to make effective investment decisions we must be aware that the value of money is not constant; but rather, it varies with ___time___ .

═══════════════════════════════

time.

2. In this study module we will consider the time value of money. The concept of "time value of money" may be defined as accounting for the accrual of compound interest over time. It may also be thought of as measuring the purchasing power of money at any point in time (past, present and future). This second concept recognizes the effects of infla-

15

tion and the subsequent value of a currency. Unless we can compare dollar values at the same point in time, we have no sound basis for making effective economic evaluation investment decisions.

What is meant by the term, time value of money?

_____

Accounting for accrued compound interest and principal or the purchasing power of money at a given point in time.

3. If you were offered $100 today or $110 in one year's time, which would you choose? To make your choice you would have to consider such factors as:

    A. If I invest $100 today, what will it be worth in a year?
    B. Is anything likely to happen to prevent my receiving the $110 in a year?

    Because the value of money varies with __time__ , such a decision (can/cannot) _____ necessarily be made with certainty.

    _____

    time, cannot

4. Suppose your choice was between $100 now and $150 in 5 years. Is the choice any more clear?

    _____

    No. Projection of other investment opportunities is necessary and projecting the future involves uncertainty.

5. To make intelligent investment decisions we must be able to compare the values of a given sum of money at different times. For example, if we could determine with certainty that $150 received in 5 years time would be worth more than $100 would grow to invested at the prevailing interest rates, then obviously, waiting 5 years is the best choice.

    At what point in time should the two sums be measured?

The easiest point in time would be either today or at the future date in 5 years because that is when one or the other of the two alternatives is known.

6. Considering the analysis at the point in time 5 years in the future, if $100 is invested at 10% for 5 years with interest compounded annually, it would earn $61 interest at the end of that time. With this investment opportunity, the better economic choice would be to _____ .

Accept the $100 now and invest it at 10% because, $161 > $150.

7. So far we have examined this problem from one future point in time. If you were to consider the analysis today, the amount you would need to invest at the same 10% interest rate to accrue $150 five years from now is less than $100. This would make the $100 today a (more/less) _____ attractive investment.

More. You could invest $100 today at 10% and accrue more than $150 after five years, since less than $100 invested today would grow to $150 in five years.

8. We have effectively compared two sums of money available at different times and established their equivalence. We compared their values at year 5 ($150 compared with $100 plus the interest earned over 5 years.) and at year 0 ($100 now compared with the sum we would have to invest today to have that money grow to $150 five years from now at a specified interest rate.) Year 0 and Year 5 are the common dates in this exercise. Either comparison could give us enough information to make a proper economic decision. Such comparisons are the only valid way to establish the time value of money.

How do you compare the value of two sums of money available at different points in time?

===

You calculate the equivalent value of each sum at a common point in time and compare the relative values directly.

9. Given three sums of money available on different dates, which dates can be used as a basis for comparison?

===

Any of the three different dates would be appropriate for comparison. However, it should be noted that these are not the only valid points in time. Any date may be used to properly determine the value of these sums of money.

10. In the preceding frames we have seen the necessity for computing future values of sums of money in order to establish the time value of those sums. This is the same as calculating the balance of a bank account earning interest, when the interest is compounded. For this reason the formula for calculating future value is referred to as the "Compound Interest Formula".

   Calculating future values is comparable to _____ .

===

Calculating compound interest plus principal.

11. "Compound interest" is always retained in the account and added to the balance, so that each interest calculation is made on a balance larger than the preceding one. This differs from "simple interest" calculations, in which the period interest is always based on the initial investment throughout the period of the investment.

   Period interest based on initial investment plus accrued interest is
   Compound interest.

===

Compound.

12. To calculate compound interest, we must know three things. The first is the sum originally invested. This is called *present value.*

    We will use letter symbols to represent the values in interest calculations. It is logical then that the letter "P" represents _____ .

    Present value.

13. We also must know the interest rate, expressed as a percentage per compounding period. Compound interest rates are represented by the letter "i". (Note that this is a lower-case or small letter "i".)

    The third thing we must know is the number of compounding periods (terms). What letter might represent this? ⌒

    "n". (Note that "n" is expressed in lower case, or small letter.)

14. Compounding terms can be of any duration but typically are in lengths of months or years.

    If interest is compounded every month for a two year investment there are ___24___ (how many) compounding terms.

    Twenty Four, (24).

15. Give the letter symbols used in interest calculations for present value, period interest rate, and the number of compounding periods.

    P = Present Value.
    i = Interest Rate.
    n = Number of Compounding Periods (terms).

16. You may also calculate the future value from a sum of money invested now. As you might expect, the letter symbol for a future sum of money is __F__ .

"F"

17. We will now examine the procedure for calculating future values from present values, and inversely, present values from future values. To graphically represent these procedures we can use a time diagram:

$$P \underline{\hspace{6cm}} F$$

$$0 \qquad 1 \qquad 2 \qquad 3 \qquad 4 \ldots\ldots n$$

The time line diagram represents an investment at time zero (now) for "n" compounding periods. If "P", "n" and the interest rate "i" are specified, can you identify "F"?

"F" is the value "n" periods in the future generated by investing "P" dollars today at an interest rate "i" per period.

18. Initial investment principal, "P", combined with interest on the sum "P", compounded for "n" terms results in the future value "F". Knowing the present sum of money to be invested, "P", and the interest rate per compounding period, "i", we can calculate "F". Suppose, however, that two compounding terms have passed. Can we still calculate the value of "F"?

Yes. The value "P" has grown by two terms of accrued interest but is still a present value, relative to the future sum "n" terms in the future. Only the value of "P" and the number of remaining compounding periods have changed.

19. Suppose we want to compare the balances at the ends of periods two and four. The following time diagrams illustrate this situation:

1)
$$P \longleftarrow F$$

| 0 | 1 | 2 | 3 | 4 ...... n |

2)
$$P \longleftarrow F$$

| 0 | 1 | 2 | 3 | 4 ...... n |

3)
$$P \longleftarrow F$$

| 0 | 1 | 2 | 3 | 4 ...... n |

To compare balances at the same point in time we must compute the values at the time chosen for comparison of the future amounts to be compared. This is referred to as "discounting" to the appropriate comparison point in time. Discounting to time zero is illustrated in diagrams 1 and 2. Discounting to period 2 is illustrated is diagram 3. The value of "P" in diagram 3 would be compared with the value of "F" in diagram 1.

What is meant by "discounting"?

━━━━━━━━━━━━━━━━━━

Computing present value(s) of future amount(s) at a point in time chosen for comparing them.

20. To review:

P = Present value, a single sum of money often, but not always, appearing at time 0 on the time line diagram.

F = Future value, a single sum of money at a designated point on the time line diagram, often at the end of project.

i = Compound interest rate.

n = The number of compounding terms over the life of the investment.

━━━━━━━━━━━━━━━━━━

No Response Required.

21. Assume an investment of $200 in a project that will yield $800 in 10 years, with interest compounded yearly. Using the above symbols;

P = _____ , F = _____ , and n = _____ .

===

$200, $800, 10.

22. Interest rates must be expressed in terms of evaluation periods involved in an analysis. For monthly evaluation periods, period interest is nominal annual interest divided by 12 months per year. Associate the following factors with their correct letter symbols:

$500 invested in a certificate of deposit today at 9% annual interest rate compounded semi-annually for 3 years.

===

P=$500, i=4.5% (9% annual interest/2 semi-annual periods per yr), n=6.

23. To determine the future value of money invested today we need to establish the proper mathematical relationship between future sums of money "F" and present sums "P". We will look at some simple formulae for doing this.

Year	0	1	2	n
Principal	P	P	$P(1+i)$	$P(1+i)^{n-1}$
+				
Interest	-	$P(i)$	$P(1+i)i$	$P(1+i)^{n-1}(i)$
=				
Accrued Balance	P	$P(1+i)$	$P(1+i)^2$	$P(1+i)^n$

In the previous table, consider the formulae under year 1. The original principal "P" earns interest during the year (Pi) and the balance at year's end is the original principal "P" plus accrued interest (Pi), stated algebraically as P(1+i).

For example, $100, "P", invested at 8.0% compounded annually, "i", earns $8 in interest during the first year, ($100)(.08). This results in an accrued balance of $108, 100+8 or 100(1+.08). At the end of year one, the balance "F" will contain the original principal plus interest earned.

Use the correct symbols to complete this formula for the balance at the end of the first year:

F = _____?_____

══════════════════════════

F = P(1+i)

24. To compute the balance at the end of year 2 we must use as "P", the balance at the end of year 1. Reading down the second column, we find "P" represented as P(1+i), which is indeed, the balance from year 1. We must multiply this by the interest rate "i" to determine the year 2 interest; this calculation is shown as P(1+i)i.

   The balance, then is the sum of the principal [P(1+i)] and interest [P(1+i)i]. This is shown in the second column as $P(1+i)^2$

   With P = $100 and i = 10%, using the above formulae, calculate the end of year balances for years 1 and 2.

══════════════════════════

Year 1 = $110, $100(1+.10)
Year 2 = $121, $110(1+.10) or $100(1+.10)^2$

25. How would you calculate the accrued balance (principal plus interest) at the beginning of year 3?

══════════════════════════

$P(1+i)^2$, The beginning of year 3 is the end of year 2.

26. Exactly the same procedure is used for column "n". The beginning principal would come from the preceding year (represented by n-1). That principal is multiplied by the interest rate and the resultant interest amount is added to the beginning principal to get the balance. Note that the balance calculation is stated in the simpler form $P(1+i)^n$.

   Assume the beginning principal is $100, with i = 8%, n = 5, compute the balance at the end of year "n", using the formulae in column "n".

═══════════════════════════════

Step (1) $P(1+i)^{n-1} = 100(1.08)^4 = 136.05$

Step (2) $P(1+i)^{n-1}(i) = 136.05(.08) = 10.88$

Step (3) $P(1+i)^{n-1} + P(1+i)^{n-1}(i) = 136.05 + 10.88 = \underline{\$146.93}$

    or $P(1+i)^n = 100(1.08)^5 = 100(1.469) = \underline{\$146.93}$

27. As we have seen, the formula for calculating the final future balance is $P(1+i)^n$. The factor $(1+i)^n$ from this formula is called the "Single Payment Compound Amount Factor", because we are calculating a future single sum of money "F" from a present single sum of money, "P". The single payment compound amount factor is designated by the factor symbol $F/P_{i,n}$.

This notation has another use, as we will see. It can be used to look up pre-computed values (for given interest rates and compounding periods) in a table that will simplify this and other time value of money factors yet to be developed.

To algebraically accomplish what is called for by the notation $F/P_{i,n}$ you would use which formula?

═══════════════════════════════

$F = P(1+i)^n$ where $(1+i)^n = F/P_{i,n}$

28. This last form of notation, $F/P_{i,n}$, is not a formula as such. When you encounter it you are simply being told to compute a future sum of money from a present sum of money at a given interest rate for a given number of compounding periods.

Now suppose that we want to calculate a present value from a future value, that is, we want to know how much we have to invest at a given rate of interest to accumulate a known amount at a future date. By mathematically rearranging the previous formula we get this expression:

$P = F/(1+i)^n$

which will calculate the desired value of "P". Note that $F/(1+i)^n$ is mathematically the same as $F[1/(1+i)^n]$. This last factor, $[1/(1+i)^n]$ is called the "Single Payment Present Worth Factor" and is designated by the factor symbol $P/F_{i,n}$. Again, this formula tells you to either use the appropriate equation or to find a specific value in a table, given the appropriate interest and compounding periods.

Identify each of the following factors with its correct name and factor symbolism:

A. $1 / (1+i)^n$

B. $(1+i)^n$

—————————————————————————————

A. Single Payment Present Worth Factor, $P/F_{i,n}$.

B. Single Payment Compound Amount Factor, $F/P_{i,n}$.

29. Without reference, write the compound interest formulae to calculate "P" given" F", and "F" given "P":

—————————————————————————————

$P = F[1/(1+i)^n]$, or $F/(1+i)^n$.

$F = P(1+i)^n$.

30. As previously mentioned, to simplify the mathematics of these calculations, the values of these factors for a wide range of interest rates and compounding periods have been pre-calculated and listed in tables. All you have to do is use the appropriate factor expression for the formula you are going to use to locate in the tables the pre-calculated value. You then use this value in place of the factor when making your calculations.

For example, to compute a present value from a future sum we could express the calculations algebraically as:

$P = F[1/(1+i)^n]$

However, a much simpler approach would be to replace the single payment present worth factor equation with its equivalent symbol, $P/F_{i,n}$ and use the tables to determine the value of the equation for specified interest and compounding periods, and compute the present value. This is illustrated as follows:

$P = F(P/F_{i,n})$

In the following table, find the correct value for the single payment present worth factor given that interest is 6% compounded annually for 8 years.

n	$F/P_{i,n}$	$P/F_{i,n}$	i = 6.00% $F/A_{i,n}$	$A/F_{i,n}$	$A/P_{i,n}$	$P/A_{i,n}$
1	1.0600	0.9434	1.0000	1.00000	1.06000	0.9434
2	1.1236	0.8900	2.0600	0.48544	0.54544	1.8334
3	1.1910	0.8396	3.1836	0.31411	0.37411	2.6730
4	1.2625	0.7921	4.3746	0.22859	0.28859	3.4651
5	1.3382	0.7473	5.6371	0.17740	0.23740	4.2124
6	1.4185	0.7050	6.9753	0.14336	0.20336	4.9173
7	1.5036	0.6651	8.3938	0.11914	0.17914	5.5824
8	1.5938	0.6274	9.8975	0.10104	0.16104	6.2098
9	1.6895	0.5919	11.4913	0.08702	0.14702	6.8017
10	1.7908	0.5584	13.1808	0.07587	0.13587	7.3601
11	1.8983	0.5268	14.9716	0.06679	0.12679	7.8869
12	2.0122	0.4970	16.8699	0.05928	0.11928	8.3838
13	2.1329	0.4688	18.8821	0.05296	0.11296	8.8527
14	2.2609	0.4423	21.0151	0.04758	0.10758	9.2950
15	2.3966	0.4173	23.2760	0.04296	0.10296	9.7122
16	2.5404	0.3936	25.6725	0.03895	0.09895	10.1059
17	2.6928	0.3714	28.2129	0.03544	0.09544	10.4773
18	2.8543	0.3503	30.9057	0.03236	0.09236	10.8276
19	3.0256	0.3305	33.7600	0.02962	0.08962	11.1581
20	3.2071	0.3118	36.7856	0.02718	0.08718	11.4699
21	3.3996	0.2942	39.9927	0.02500	0.08500	11.7641
22	3.6035	0.2775	43.3923	0.02305	0.08305	12.0416
23	3.8197	0.2618	46.9958	0.02128	0.08128	12.3034
24	4.0489	0.2470	50.8156	0.01968	0.07968	12.5504
25	4.2919	0.2330	54.8645	0.01823	0.07823	12.7834
26	4.5494	0.2198	59.1564	0.01690	0.07690	13.0032
27	4.8223	0.2074	63.7058	0.01570	0.07570	13.2105
28	5.1117	0.1956	68.5281	0.01459	0.07459	13.4062
29	5.4184	0.1846	73.6398	0.01358	0.07358	13.5907
30	5.7435	0.1741	79.0582	0.01265	0.07265	13.7648
31	6.0881	0.1643	84.8017	0.01179	0.07179	13.9291
32	6.4534	0.1550	90.8898	0.01100	0.07100	14.0840
33	6.8406	0.1462	97.3432	0.01027	0.07027	14.2302
34	7.2510	0.1379	104.1838	0.00960	0.06960	14.3681
35	7.6861	0.1301	111.4348	0.00897	0.06897	14.4982
36	8.1473	0.1227	119.1209	0.00839	0.06839	14.6210
37	8.6361	0.1158	127.2681	0.00786	0.06786	14.7368
38	9.1543	0.1092	135.9042	0.00736	0.06736	14.8460
39	9.7035	0.1031	145.0585	0.00689	0.06689	14.9491
40	10.2857	0.0972	154.7620	0.00646	0.06646	15.0463
48	16.3939	0.0610	256.5645	0.00390	0.06390	15.6500
50	18.4202	0.0543	290.3359	0.00344	0.06344	15.7619

$P/F_{6\%,8} = [1/(1+.06)]^8 = 0.6274$

31. In addition to the 6% interest rate table and the tables at the end of this manual, expanded tables for interest rates from 0.5% to 200% and a range of compounding periods may be found in Appendix A of Stermole and Stermole's text, "Economic Evaluation and Investment Decision Methods", 8th Edition. In working with the compound interest rate tables it is important to recognize that "n" represents the number of compounding periods involved over time. Further, the period interest rate is determined by dividing the annual interest rate by the number of compounding periods per year. Therefore, if we had an annual interest rate of 12% that was compounded semi-annually (twice a year) the desired period interest rate would be 12%/2 = 6%.

Using the previous table, determine the value of the $P/F_{i,n}$ factor for an interest rate of 12.0% compounded semi-annually, over 5 years.

Period Interest Rate = 12%/2 = 6%
Compounding Periods = (5 years)(2 semi-annual periods per year) = 10
$P/F_{6\%,10} = 0.5584$

32. If, in Frame 31, we had a future value 5 years from now (10 semi-annual compounding periods) of $500, determine the equivalent present value for a 6% semi-annual period interest rate.

500(0.5584) = 279.2 = P

33. Following are six examples of the use of the formulae you have learned, each followed by a problem for you to solve. Study the examples carefully; then work the accompanying exercise. Don't look at the solutions before you have made every effort to work the problem. If your solution is wrong, review the frames dealing with the pertinent material and then try the problem again.

Again, the tables you will use in solving these problems may be found at the back of this text, or Appendix A in the reference text, "Economic Evaluation and Investment Decision Methods", 8th Edition, 1993, by Stermole and Stermole. You may also hand calculate the needed factors using the y^x function available on most calculators.

34. Calculate the value of $100 invested now in a bank account earning 10% interest compounded annually for one year.

Using a line diagram we obtain:

$P = \$100$ $F = ?$

0   1

$P = 100$
$i = 10.0\%$
$n = 1$
$F = P(1+i)^n$ or $F = P(F/P_{i,n})$

Therefore,

$F = 100(1.1) = 110.$

35. A man wants to buy a car for $15,000 and price escalation is estimated to be 20% per year. What will the price be if he waits for a year to purchase the car?

$$1.200$$
$$\$15,000(F/P_{20\%,1}) = \$18,000$$

36. A man is offered a job paying $20,000 per year and he is told this salary offer is 6% above the salary paid for this position one year ago. What was the salary for this position one year ago?

Using a line diagram we obtain:

P = ?   \$20,000

0   1 year

F = \$20,000

i = 6.0%

n = 1

P = ?

Therefore; $P + P(0.06) = P(1+.06) = \$20,000$, or

$P = \$20,000(1/(1+.06)^1)$ or $P = \$20,000(P/F_{6\%,1})$

$P = \$20,000(0.9434) = \$18,870$

37. A man wishes to buy a washing machine costing \$600. He then sees a sign advertising the washing machine "At last year's price". If inflation last year was 15.0%, what might you expect the price of the machine to be?

        .8696

$\$600(P/F_{15\%,1}) = \$521.70$

38. Calculate the future value of \$100 in 5 years time if it is invested now at 15.0% per year.

Using a line diagram we obtain:

\$100   F = ?

0   1   2   3   4   5

$F = P(F/P_{i\%,n}) = P(1+i)^n = \$100(1+.15)^5 = \$100(2.011) = \$201.10$

           2.011

$F = \$100(F/P_{15\%,5}) = \$201.10$

39. Calculate the future value of \$150 in 8 years time if it is invested now at 10% per year.

━━━━━━━━━━━━━━━━━━━━━━━━

$$2.144$$
$$F = \$150(F/P_{10\%,8}) = \$321.60$$

40. Calculate the present value at year 0 and future value at the end of year 8 of $250 to be received at the end of year 3, if interest rate is 15.0% per year.

━━━━━━━━━━━━━━━━━━━━━━━━

Using a line diagram we obtain:

P = ?		$250					F = ?	
0	1	2	3	4	5	6	7	8

$$.6575$$
$$P = \$250(P/F_{15\%,3}) = \$164.40$$

$$2.011$$
$$F = \$250(F/P_{15\%,5}) = \$502.80$$

$$3.059$$
$$\text{or } F = \$164.4(F/P_{15\%,8}) = \$502.80$$

The two solutions for calculating "F" may vary slightly due to round-off error on the number of significant figures you carry on the F/P factors located in the textbook Appendix A tables.

41. Calculate the sum that invested now, will achieve a balance of $500 in 5 years time at an interest rate of 10% per year. Also, what would be the accrued balance after 15 years?

━━━━━━━━━━━━━━━━━━━━━━━━

P = ?	—	—	F=$500	—	F=?
0	1 4		5	6 15	

$$.6209$$
$$P = \$500(P/F_{10\%,5}) = \$310.40$$

$$2.594$$
$$F = \$500(F/P_{10\%,10}) = \$1,297$$

$$4.177$$
$$\text{or } F = \$310.4(F/P_{10\%,15}) = \$1,297$$

42. The future and present values of single lump sum payments, which we have been studying, are a part of any project, but they are not the only considerations. In economic evaluation problems we sometimes encounter *uniform series* of equal values and may be required to compute the compounded (future value) or discounted (present worth) amount of such a series. Or we might want to calculate the amount of a uniform series of equal end-of-period payments that are equivalent to a future or present sum.

We will now introduce the term "A", which represents a uniform series of equal values. Essentially, the letter "A" stands for "annual" because often compounding periods are on an annual basis. But in our formulae, "A" simply stands for a series of equivalent values to be realized uniformly over time at a series of evaluation periods which might be days, months, quarters or years.

The term "A" represents a series of equivalent values occurring over compounding periods of (months/years) _____ .

Both, either months or years may be appropriate.

43. The following line diagram illustrates the series of equal values concept for future value analysis.

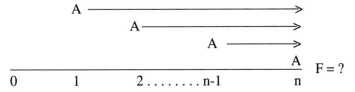

A series of equal investments, each represented by an "A", is made with each investment being made at a different period. Thus each single investment draws interest for a different number of compounding periods. The investment "A" made at the end of period "n" draws no interest, the investment at period n-1 draws interest for 1 period.

Assuming n = 4 in the above diagram, which investment will draw interest for three periods?

━━━━━━━━━━━━━━━━━━━━━━━━

The investment made at period 1.

44. There is a formula which will compute the cumulative future worth of all these investments. The formula is:

$F = A[(1+i)^n-1]/i$

This equation is referred to as the "Uniform Series Compound Amount Factor" and the factor is designated by the factor symbol $(F/A_{i\%,n})$.

Note: The derivation of this equation and the remaining ones in this module are illustrated in the Stermole and Stermole text previously referenced. For purposes of this manual we are interested only in the proper application of these factors in making economic evaluations.

Without reference, write the compound interest formula to calculate "F" given "A":

━━━━━━━━━━━━━━━━━━━━━━━━

$F = A[(1+i)^n-1]/i$

45. Calculate the future value 6 years from now given a uniform series of $1,000 investments made at the end of each year for the next 6 years if the interest rate is 10.0% per year compounded annually. Use the tables or calculate the factor needed from the definition in Frame 44.

—	A=$1,000	A=$1,000	A=$1,000	F= ?
0	1	2 6		

━━━━━━━━━━━━━━━━━━━━━━━━

7.716
$F = \$1,000(F/A_{10\%,6}) = \$7,716$

where $F/A_{10,6} = [(1+.10)^6-1]/.10 = 7.716$

46. The $(F/A_{i,n})$ factor and the remaining three factors to be developed in this section represent short cuts for discounting when we have series of equivalent values. As an alternative to using the $(F/A_{i,n})$ we could utilize "n-1" $(F/P_{i,n})$ factors and sum the results to determine the net future value. Obviously the use of a single factor is much more convenient when making hand calculations.

In Frame 45, how many $(F/P_{i,n})$ factors would be required to calculate the future value "F"?

Five (5). As illustrated mathematically below, the last value in year 6 does not accrue any interest so it is added to the other compounded amounts to determine the future worth:

$$F = 1,000 + 1,000(F/P_{10,1}) + 1,000(F/P_{10,2}) + 1,000(F/P_{10,3})$$
$$+ 1,000(F/P_{10,4}) + 1,000(F/P_{10,5}) = 7,716$$

47. Additional time value of money factors that you should be familiar with are presented in the following frames. Each involves a uniform series of values. The first factor is the inverse of $(F/A_{i,n})$ factor that was discussed in the preceding frames. Mathematically, this is defined as:

$A = F[i/\{(1+i)^n-1\}]$

This factor is referred to as the "Sinking Fund Deposit Factor" and is designated by the factor symbolism $(A/F_{i,n})$. Identify the table value for the sinking fund deposit factor, $(A/F_{i,n})$ given that "i" equals 6.0% per annum for a 10 year project. The appropriate table is located on page 26 of this manual or in Appendix A of the Stermole and Stermole text.

0.07587, where $A/F_{6,10} = 0.06 / [(1+.06)^{10}-1] = 0.07587$

48. Calculate the uniform series of equal payments made at the end of each year for 10 years that are equivalent to a $1000 payment 10 years from now if the interest is 6% compounded annually.

$$\frac{\overset{A=?}{0} \quad \overset{A=?}{1} \quad \overset{A=?}{2} \quad \overset{A=? \ldots \ldots A=?}{3 \ldots \ldots \ldots 10}}{} \quad F=\$1,000$$

$$.07587$$
$$A = \$1000(A/F_{6\%,10}) = \$75.87$$

49. Another uniform series calculation you might have to make involves the "Capital Recovery Factor". This calculation determines a uniform series of end of period payments, "A", that are equivalent to a present single sum of money, "P". Mathematically the formula is:

$$A = P[i(1+i)^n/(1+i)^n-1]$$

The capital recovery factor is expressed by the factor symbol $(A/P_{i,n})$.

Calculate the uniform series of payments at the end of each year for 6 years, that are equivalent to a present sum of $1000 if interest is 10.0% per year compounded annually. The problem is presented on the following time diagram and illustrates your basic mortgage payment calculation.

$$\begin{array}{cccccc} P=\$1,000 & A=? & A=? & A=? \ldots \ldots A=? \\ 0 & 1 & 2 & 3 \ldots \ldots \ldots 6 \end{array}$$

$$.22961$$
$$A = \$1,000(A/P_{10\%,6}) = \$229.61$$

50. Given that P = $10,000, i = 6%, and n = 15, solve for "A" using the appropriate factor and value from the 6% interest rate table on page 26.

$$.10296$$
$$A = \$10,000(A/P_{6\%,15}) = \$1,029.60$$

51. The final formula associated with uniform series is used to calculate a present single sum of money "P" that is equivalent to a uniform series of equal end of period payments. The formula is mathematically defined as:

$$P = A[(1+i)^n-1]/[i(1+i)^n]$$

This formula is defined as the "Uniform Series Present Worth Factor" and is expressed by the factor symbol $(P/A_{i,n})$.

Calculate the year 0 present value of a series of $1000 payments to be made at the end of each year for 6 years, if interest is 10% per year compounded annually.

P=? $\dfrac{\quad A{=}\$1000 \quad A{=}\$1000 \quad A{=}\$1000 \ldots\ldots A{=}\$1000}{\ 0 \qquad 1 \qquad\quad 2 \qquad\quad 3\ldots\ldots\ldots\ldots 6}$

$$P = \$1000(P/A_{10\%,6}) = \$4,355$$

$$\text{where } P/A_{10\%,6} = [(1+.10)^6-1]/[.10(1+.10)^6] = 4.355$$

52. Note that the uniform series present worth factor in the previous exercise $(P/A_{10\%,6})$ discounts the six $1000 values to time zero (which is the beginning of the first year for which there is a value) and not to the end of period 1.

This concludes Module 2. A summary of all compound interest formulae is given in Section 2.2 of the reference text. The criterion test for this module is presented on the following page.

53. Present, Future and Annual Values, Criterion Test:

Using either the tables, or hand calculation of factors, A) Correctly calculate what sum of money must be invested now at an interest rate of 15.0% compounded annually, to achieve a balance of $200 in 2 years time; B) then calculate what equal annual payments at years 1 and 2 would be equivalent to receiving $200 two years from now; C) finally, calculate the value that the $200 to be received in two years would grow to 10 years from now for the same interest rates.

Present, Future, Annual Value, Criterion Test Solution:

$$F = \$200$$

P = ? $\underline{\qquad A = ?\qquad A = ?\qquad\qquad\qquad\qquad\qquad}$ F = ?

    0   1   2   3   4 10

A) P $= \$200(P/F_{15\%,2}) = \$151.22$
                 .7561

B) A $= \$200(A/F_{15\%,2}) = \$93.02$
                 .46512

    or

A $= \$151.22(A/P_{15\%,2}) = \$93.02$
                 .61512

C) F $= \$200(F/P_{15\%,8}) = \$611.80$
                 3.059

    or

F $= \$151.22(F/P_{15\%,10}) = \$611.80$
                 4.046

MODULE 3

Net Present Value (NPV)

1. In the preceding study modules in this course we have learned about two elements that are vital to project evaluation. They are:

   A) Cash Flow
   B) The Time Value of Money

   We saw that cash flow is the movement of money into and out of a company's accounts. Inward or positive cash flow comes from sales revenues, earned interest, dividends, salvage revenues, etc. Outward, or negative cash flow results from expenditures such as research, exploration, development, operating costs, administrative expenses, etc.

   If inward cash flow exceeds outward we have _____ cash flow. If the opposite is true, we have _____ cash flow.

   ═══════════════════════════════

   positive,
   negative

2. We also learned about the time value of money. We learned that the value or purchasing power of money varies with time and that to compare two sums of money available at different times we must establish their respective values at a common point in time or spread the values uniformly over the same periods.

   Using today as a comparison point for two or more sums of money is often referred to as what time on a time line diagram?_____.

Time zero or the present. Remember that for comparison purposes time zero can be anywhere on a cash flow line diagram.

3. The minimum rate of return, whose symbol is "i*", is often referred to as the opportunity cost of capital. Both terms represent alternative investment opportunities that must be passed by if capital is invested elsewhere. The terms hurdle rate and discount rate also are used interchangeably with minimum rate of return and have exactly the same meaning. Opportunity cost of capital is synonymous with _____ _____.

Minimum Rate of Return.

4. In this module we will combine the concepts of cash flow and the time value of money to introduce the first of several decision criteria used in economic evaluations. This concept is defined as net present value or (NPV).

    Net Present Value, (NPV) is defined as the cumulative value of all project cash flows, (positive and negative) discounted at the minimum rate of return, (or hurdle rate) to the present.

    With NPV we normally are placing a value on a project's future cash flows at what point in time?

Time zero or the present.

5. Mathematically NPV is represented as follows:

    NPV = PW Positive Cash Flow @ i* + PW Negative Cash Flow @ i*

    Where "PW" represents "Present Worth" or "discounted" and "i*" is defined as the minimum rate of return, or discount rate, we are willing to accept for this project, because we believe we have other places where money can be invested to earn at least this amount of return.

Project cash flows are _____ at the minimum rate of return to compute the project net present value (NPV).

━━━━━━━━━━━━━━━━━━━━━━━━━━━━━

discounted.

6. Often in describing NPV the terms "revenue" and "costs" are used inter-changeably with positive and negative cash flow. In computing NPV, costs are measured in absolute value and subtracted from revenues. But to emphasize the use of after-tax cash flows in economic evaluations, NPV has been specifically defined on a cash flow basis. NPV can be defined as the cumulative value of _____ cash flows associated with a project or investment.

━━━━━━━━━━━━━━━━━━━━━━━━━━━━━

discounted positive and negative

7. Example of Net Present Value, (NPV). Given the following proposal (in millions of dollars) to improve an existing process, calculate the NPV of the project, given that $i^* = 15.0\%$.

$$\frac{C=\$50 \qquad\qquad I=\$50 \qquad\qquad\qquad I=\$50}{0 \qquad\qquad\qquad 1 \ldots\ldots\ldots\ldots 5} \; L=\$50$$

Where; C = Cost, I = Savings, L = Salvage. Both "I" and "L" represent positive cash flow which are to be discounted. The only cost associated with this project occurs at time zero and is currently a present value. This solution involves the use of the single payment present worth factor and the uniform series present worth factor.

━━━━━━━━━━━━━━━━━━━━━━━━━━━━━

$$\qquad\qquad 3.352 \qquad\qquad .4972$$
$$NPV = \$50(P/A_{15\%,5}) + \$50(P/F_{15\%,5}) - \$50 = +\$142.46$$

8. In the above equation for calculating the project NPV, what does the uniform series present worth factor $(P/A_{15\%,5})$ accomplish?

It computes the present worth at time zero of the five revenues realized in years one through five. In this case time zero is the beginning of the first period for which there is a value. The first revenue occurs at the end of year one, so the revenues are brought back to the beginning of year one (time zero).

9. Referring to the same NPV equation, what does the single payment present worth factor $(P/F_{15\%,5})$ accomplish and why do we then subtract $50?

The factor $P/F_{15\%,5}$ computes the present worth at time zero of the salvage value realized at the end of year five. $50 is subtracted because this sum is the present worth of the capital cost invested at the beginning of the project's life. The investment of this sum will generate the future savings (income) and the final salvage value.

10. To utilize NPV in economic evaluation decision-making you must know how to interpret the meaning of NPV results. NPV results greater than zero (0) indicate that the project is acceptable and in fact, is earning a compound interest rate in excess of the minimum rate of return, or discount rate. When NPV is equal to zero (0), the project is said to be a breakeven with investing elsewhere at the minimum rate of return. If the NPV is negative, the project is unsatisfactory indicating we would be better off investing available funds elsewhere at the minimum rate of return.

    Is a project with a zero NPV acceptable? (Yes, No, Maybe)

Yes. It is a breakeven with investing elsewhere at the minimum rate of return.

11. Interpret the meaning of the net present value of +$142.46 calculated in the example in Frame 7.

═══════════════════════════════════════

NPV of +$142.46 indicates acceptable economics since NPV > 0. We could afford to invest an additional $142.46 in this project in the year the NPV has been calculated and still expect to receive the minimum rate of return on invested dollars.

12. When evaluating numerous investments from which only one alternative may be selected, (mutually exclusive alternatives), we always select the project with the largest positive net present value (NPV) because incremental analysis of mutually exclusive alternatives always leads to selecting the project with maximum NPV on total investment as the economic choice.

If we are looking at 5 different development plans for a proposed project and only one plan can be selected for development, what is the proper criterion for selecting the economically optimal design?

═══════════════════════════════════════

Largest Positive NPV.

13. If we are interested in selecting more than one investment from a pool of projects that may be available, (non-mutually exclusive alternatives) then we need to look at a value other than the largest NPV. *When selecting more than one project, we need to select the group of projects that provide the largest cumulative net present value we can obtain from the investment of available capital. This does not imply that we always select the project with the largest individual NPV! Several small projects often give more cumulative NPV for given budget dollars than the project or projects with largest individual project NPV.*

Cumulative NPV is just the total NPV obtained from proceeding with more than one project. It is calculated by adding up the individual project NPV's selected. Obviously, projects with negative NPV would not be considered since these do not have satisfactory economics relative to investing elsewhere at the minimum discount rate.

If we are looking at 5 independent mining, drilling or real estate ventures from which only 2 or 3 may be selected due to budget restrictions, how do we determine which projects to select from an economic viewpoint?

Calculate individual project NPV(s) and select the group of projects that will maximize cumulative NPV for available investment capital. This may or may not involve the project with the largest NPV.

14. A company has $200,000 available for three different projects. Three projects, each with 6 year lives are being considered with expected costs, incomes and expenses as follows:

Project	Year 0 Investment	Year 1-6 Annual Incomes	Year 1-6 Annual Expenses	Year 6 Salvage Value
1	$50,000	$60,000	$20,000	$40,000
2	$150,000	$90,000	$35,000	$50,000
3	$200,000	$125,000	$50,000	$70,000

Any money that is not invested in one of the projects will be invested elsewhere in the company for process improvements estimated to give a 10% return. Determine the optimum way to invest the $200,000 to maximize the total investment profitability using NPV analysis.

Solution, (In Thousands of Dollars):

Note: The discount rate in this problem is represented by the other opportunities that are thought to exist for the investment of available capital, or in this case, 10.0%. Further, since the annual income and expenses occur at the same point in time, these values can be netted together prior to computing the net present values to simplify calculations.

Project 1

$$\text{NPV} = \$40(P/A_{10\%,6}) + \$40(P/F_{10\%,6}) - \$50 = +\$146.78$$

(4.355) (.5645)

Project 2

$$\text{NPV} = \$55(P/A_{10\%,6}) + \$50(P/F_{10\%,6}) - \$150 = +\$117.75$$

(4.355) (.5645)

Project 3

$$\text{NPV} = \$75(P/A_{10\%,6}) + \$70(P/F_{10\%,6}) - \$200 = +\$166.14$$

(4.355) (.5645)

Since more than one project may be selected with the available capital, choose projects 1 and 2 to maximize NPV. Projects 1 and 2 generate +$264.53 of NPV for $200 thousand invested, while project 3 generates +$166.14 thousand for the same invested capital. Note this does not involve selecting project 3 with maximum individual project NPV.

15. Calculate the NPV for the following two unequal life alternatives for a minimum rate of return of 20%, and decide which option is the most viable if only one project may be selected (mutually exclusive analysis).

I = Profit, L = Salvage, C = Cost.

A) $\dfrac{\text{C=\$88} \qquad\qquad \text{I=\$35} \qquad\qquad\qquad\qquad\qquad \text{I=\$35}}{0 \qquad\qquad\qquad\qquad 1\ldots\ldots\ldots\ldots\ldots\ldots\ldots\ldots\ldots\ldots 5}$

B) $\dfrac{\text{C=\$50} \qquad \text{I=\$30} \qquad\qquad \text{I=\$30} \qquad\quad — \qquad\quad —}{0 \qquad\qquad\quad 1\ldots\ldots\ldots\ldots 3 \qquad\quad 4 \qquad\quad 5}$

Solution: When income-producing alternatives have different lives, assume they have equal lives equivalent to the longest life alternative with zero revenues and costs in the latter years of the shorter life alternative.

A) NPV = $35(P/A_{20\%,5})$ - $88 = +$16.7

B) NPV = $30(P/A_{20\%,3})$ - $50 = +$13.2

Therefore, select alternative "A" as the most economical mutually exclusive alternative as it has the largest NPV.

16. It should be pointed out that the user is not limited to evaluations on a present value basis. As was illustrated in the present, future, annual value module, we can determine the value of a stream of cash flows at any point in time. Therefore, we are not limited to Net Present Value, (NPV) but can also calculate Net Annual Value, (NAV) or Net Future Value, (NFV) depending on user preference. Typically, we want to know the value of a project today, so NPV is the predominant calculation, but other available techniques are equally valid and will consistently lead to the same economic conclusion if applied properly. It is important to recognize when using methods other than present value, that if project lives vary, using annual value or future value will require some careful con-

sideration since values must be established over the same life for annual analysis and at the same future point in time for net future value analysis. List the three types of value analyses that can be made in economic evaluations.

Net Present Value, (NPV), Net Annual Value, (NAV), Net Future Value, (NFV)

17. In performing net value analyses on a given project there is one additional aspect you might have to consider. This concerns the project's expected life. Normally extending a project life beyond 10 or 15 years will have minimal effect on economic analysis results. But for those projects whose lives are less than 10 years, the selection of the project life can significantly affect the economics not only for NPV, but for all economic decision criteria.

When should you be concerned about project life projections in economic evaluations?

Typically, when the project life is less than 10 years.

18. The following example shows two different levels of improvement being considered for an existing process. The new equipment costs and projected annual savings in labor and materials are:

	Equipment Cost	Projected Annual Savings
Level 1	$200,000	$125,000
Level 2	$350,000	$180,000

For i* = 20%, evaluate Levels 1 and 2 using NPV analysis assuming zero salvage value for:

A) 3 Year Evaluation Life
B) 5 Year Evaluation Life

Solution in Thousands of Dollars.

Case A, 3 Year Evaluation:

$$\text{Level 1, NPV} = \$125(P/A_{20\%,3}) - \$200 = +\$63.25$$
$$\overset{2.106}{}$$

$$\text{Level 2, NPV} = \$180(P/A_{20\%,3}) - \$350 = +\$29.08$$
$$\overset{2.106}{}$$

Therefore, for a 3 year life, select Level 1 with maximum NPV since the alternatives are mutually exclusive.

Case B, 5 Year Evaluation;

$$\text{Level 1, NPV} = \$125(P/A_{20\%,5}) - \$200 = +\$173.88$$
$$\overset{2.991}{}$$

$$\text{Level 2, NPV} = \$180(P/A_{20\%,5}) - \$350 = +\$188.38$$
$$\overset{2.991}{}$$

Therefore, for a 5 year life, select Level 2. Note that the economic choice has switched for a 5 year life compared to a 3 year life.

19. It is proposed to achieve labor cost savings on a production process by installing one of two possible equipment automation changes. New capital equipment costs and projected savings (cash flow) are as follows:

	Equipment Cost	Projected Annual Savings
Change 1	$150,000	$80,000
Change 2	$230,000	$115,000

Which change, if either, should be selected if $i^* = 40\%$? Use NPV analysis and assume zero salvage values for an evaluation life of A) 6 years and B) 8 years.

Case A, Six Year Life Analysis:

Change 1 NPV = +$23,440, Select Change 1.

Change 2 NPV = +$19,320

Case B, Eight Year Life Analysis:

Change 1 NPV = +$36,480

Change 2 NPV = +$38,065, Select Change 2.

20. To summarize briefly, we have learned that Net Present Value analysis provides a quick, easy and therefore, very useful way of screening multiple mutually exclusive project alternatives to determine which is best. Finally, remember that a project earning at the minimum rate of return, "i*", has a zero net value, so projects with a positive NPV are better than investing money elsewhere at "i*". Since time zero is common to all alternatives regardless of project life, unequal project lives do not affect NPV analysis. However, unequal project lives must be properly considered when net annual values (NAV) or net future values (NFV) are utilized. This means looking at equal equivalent lives for annual value and comparing future values at the same future point in time, regardless of when a project may be expected to terminate. List the forms of value analysis that require careful consideration of project life.

―――――――――――――――――――――――

Net Annual Value, (NAV), Net Future Value, (NFV).

21. Several work exercises follow to assess your understanding of NPV calculations and the evaluation of project alternatives based on NPV analysis.

22. Consider the following 4 investment alternatives which all have a 5 year life and zero salvage value. Assume that i* = 20%.

Alternative	Investment, $	Savings/Year, $
1	10,000	6,000
2	25,000	10,000
3	35,000	15,000
4	50,000	17,000

Which single alternative should be selected if $50,000 is available for investment and the alternatives are mutually exclusive improvement projects?

Alt. 1, NPV = $6,000(P/A_{20,5}) - 10,000 = +\$7,946$
Alt. 2, NPV = $10,000(P/A_{20,5}) - 25,000 = +\$4,910$
Alt. 3, NPV = $15,000(P/A_{20,5}) - 35,000 = +\$9,865$
Alt. 4, NPV = $17,000(P/A_{20,5}) - 50,000 = +\$\ 847$

Select Alternative 3 and invest the remaining \$15,000 elsewhere at $i* = 20\%$ to give NPV = 0. This gives more cumulative NPV for your \$50,000 budget than any other choice.

23. If more than one alternative could be selected because the alternatives in frame 22 are non-mutually exclusive (independent), which alternatives would be chosen?

Selecting alternatives one and three involves investing \$45,000 and gives the most cumulative NPV (+\$17,811) for the available budget of \$50,000. The remaining \$5,000 not invested in these alternatives would be invested at the minimum rate of return and have zero NPV.

24. Two unequal life investment alternatives "A" and "B" from which only one may be selected, must be evaluated to determine the best economic choice for $i* = 20\%$. The investments C, incomes I, and salvage values L, are shown on the time diagrams in thousands of dollars.

A) $\dfrac{\text{C=\$100} \quad \text{I=\$40} \quad \text{I=\$40} \dots\dots\dots\dots \text{I=\$40}}{0 \qquad\quad 1 \qquad\quad 2 \dots\dots\dots\dots\dots 5}$ L=\$100

B) $\dfrac{\text{C=\$150} \quad \text{I=\$60} \quad \text{I=\$60} \quad \text{I=\$60}}{0 \qquad\quad 1 \qquad\quad 2 \qquad\quad 3}$ L=\$150

Evaluate the mutually exclusive projects using NPV analysis.

A) NPV = +\$59.8
B) NPV = +\$63.2, Select Alternative "B" with the largest NPV.

25. A friend offers to give you 4 payments of $1,000 at annual time periods shown on the diagram if you will give him $5,000 three years from now. Your minimum rate of return is 20%.

			C=$5,000
I=$1,000	I=$1,000	I=$1,000	I=$1,000
0	1	2	3

   A) Evaluate this economic opportunity shown on the time diagram using NPV analysis as to whether or not you would accept your friends offer?

   B) If you were to repay him $6,000 instead of $5,000 three years from now would you accept his offer?

   _____

   A) $NPV = 1,000 + 1,000(P/A_{20,3}) - 5,000(P/F_{20,3})$
      $= +$213$, Accept offer.
   B) $NPV = 1,000 + 1,000(P/A_{20,3}) - 6,000(P/F_{20,3})$
      $= -$366$, Reject offer.

26. A new process can be developed and operated at Levels "A" or "B" with capital costs, sales and operating costs as shown;

	Life (Yrs)	Yr 0 Capital Investment	Annual Sales	Annual Op. Costs
Level A	5	100	75	35
Level B	5	150	100	45

   Assuming $i* = 20\%$, and there is zero salvage value at the end of the life of each process, which level of investment should be selected? Use NPV analysis.

   _____

   Level A, $NPV = 40(P/A_{20,5}) - 100 = +19.6
   Level B, $NPV = 55(P/A_{20,5}) - 150 = +14.5
   Select Level "A" with maximum NPV because the alternatives are mutually exclusive.

27. Criterion Test for Net Present Value Module.

The following three unequal life investment alternatives with costs, profits and salvage values shown on the time diagrams in thousands of dollars are being considered.

A) $\dfrac{\text{C=\$160} \qquad\qquad \text{I=\$150.}\dots\dots\dots\dots\dots\dots \text{I=\$150}}{0 \qquad\qquad\qquad 1 \dots\dots\dots\dots\dots\dots\dots\dots\dots 5}$ L=\$50

B) $\dfrac{\text{C=\$320} \qquad\qquad \text{I=\$275.}\dots\dots\dots\dots \text{I=\$275}}{0 \qquad\qquad\qquad 1\dots\dots\dots\dots\dots\dots 4}$ L=\$70

C) $\dfrac{\text{C=\$480} \qquad\qquad \text{I=\$500}\dots\dots \text{I=\$500}}{0 \qquad\qquad\qquad 1\dots\dots\dots\dots 3}$ L=\$100

Assuming $480 is available to invest and other opportunities exist to invest all available dollars at a 20% minimum rate of return. Use NPV analysis to:

A) Determine which of the alternatives is the most viable proposition if the alternatives are different ways of developing the same project and only one alternative may be selected (mutually exclusive alternatives).

B) Determine which alternatives are the most viable if the alternatives all represent different independent projects so more than one alternative may be selected (non-mutually exclusive alternatives).

Solution to NPV Module, Criterion Test:

Case A)

$$\overset{2.991}{\text{A, NPV}} = 150(P/A_{20\%,5}) + \overset{.4019}{50(P/F_{20\%,5})} - 160 = +\$308.7$$

$$\overset{2.589}{\text{B, NPV}} = 275(P/A_{20\%,4}) + \overset{.4823}{70(P/F_{20\%,4})} - 320 = +\$425.7$$

$$\overset{2.106}{\text{C, NPV}} = 500(P/A_{20\%,3}) + \overset{.5787}{100(P/F_{20\%,3})} - 480 = +\$630.9$$

Therefore, select Alternative "C", with the largest NPV since the alternatives are mutually exclusive in Case A).

Case B)

The alternatives are non-mutually exclusive so maximize cumulative NPV rather than an individual project NPV. Select Alternatives "A" & "B" to maximize cumulative NPV for budget of $480. This gives value of +$734.4 which is greater than +$630.9 from "C" alone for same dollars invested.

MODULE 4

Present Value Ratio, PVR

1. In the preceding modules in this course you have learned about:

   A) Cash Flow
   B) The time value of money and how to calculate it using specific formulae.
   C) The discounted cash flow analysis technique of NPV (net present value) which is calculated in terms of "i*", the minimum rate of return.

   In this module you will learn another technique to assist you in project evaluation. Present value ratio is the ratio of project NPV to present worth investment calculated at "i*".

   You will recall that in Module 3, we defined net present value as
   _____ .

   ═══════════════════════════

   The sum of the present values of each year's projected cash flow during the life of the project, discounted at "i*".

2. And, "i*" was defined as _____ .

   ═══════════════════════════

   The minimum rate of return an investor can accept from an investment since he has other investments that can earn at least that level of interest. It is also referred to as the opportunity cost of capital, hurdle rate, or discount rate.

3. Present Value Ratio, (PVR) is defined as the ratio of the project NPV to
    the absolute value of present worth net investment costs not offset by
    revenue (negative cash flow). It is important to recognize that on an
    after-tax basis, investment costs are equivalent to negative cash flow.
    Mathematically, the present worth of net costs equals the absolute value
    (the positive value) of discounted negative cash flow. |Present Worth
    Negative Cash Flow| means absolute value (positive value) of the pre-
    sent worth negative cash flow which equals present worth of net costs
    not offset by revenues.

    Write the fraction that represents the ratio we want to calculate.

    _____

    ═══════════════════════════════

    $$\frac{\text{Net Present Value}}{|\text{Present Worth Negative Cash Flow}|} \quad \text{or} \quad \frac{\text{Net Present Value}}{|\text{Present Worth Net Costs}|}$$

4. Net Present Value and the term "Present Worth Net Investment Costs"
    or "negative cash flow", imply discounting at the minimum rate of
    return. This means that both the numerator and denominator incorporate
    the time value of money in this ratio. To accomplish this we must dis-
    count both numerator and denominator by handling the time value of
    money using an interest rate equal to _____.

    ═══════════════════════════════

    "i*", the minimum rate of return.

5. To show how we develop the numerator and denominator for PVR cal-
    culations we will use the following project presented on the time line
    diagram, with i* = 10%. If you have problems with the numerator calcu-
    lations you should review the material in Module 3, on NPV.

    $$\frac{\text{C=\$20,000} \qquad \text{I=\$5,000} \ldots \ldots \ldots \text{I=\$5,000}}{0 \qquad\qquad\qquad 1 \ldots \ldots \ldots \ldots \ldots 7} \quad \text{L=\$20,000}$$

    $$\qquad\qquad\quad 4.868 \qquad\qquad .5132$$
    $$\text{NPV} = \$5,000(P/A_{10\%,7}) + \$20,000(P/F_{10\%,7}) - \$20,000 = +\$14,605$$

What do the expressions $(P/A_{10\%,7})$ and $(P/F_{10\%,7})$ accomplish in this NPV equation?

——————

This equation uses the *uniform series present worth factor* $(P/A_{10\%,7})$ to calculate the present worth of the income $(I=\$5,000)$ from each of the 7 periods of the project's life back to the beginning of the first period for which there is a value. The beginning of year 1 is time zero. The *single payment present worth factor* $(P/F_{10\%,7})$ calculates the present worth of the salvage revenue, $(L=\$20,000)$ realized at the end of year 7 brought back to time zero.

6. The denominator for PVR is the present worth investment cost not offset by project revenue, discounted at "i^*". What does the line diagram in Frame 5 show as investment costs?

——————

$20,000. (The initial cost located at time zero.)

7. Does this sum have to be converted to present worth? Why?

——————

No. Since the investment cost is realized at time zero, it is already a present value.

8. Calculate the present value ratio for the project in Frame 5.

——————

$PVR = +\$14,605 / \$20,000 = +0.73$

9. It should be obvious that as long as a project has a positive net present value, the calculated PVR will always be greater than zero. Therefore, PVR calculations indicate satisfactory economics whenever the ratio is

greater than zero. PVR's equal to zero are a breakeven with investing elsewhere, while PVR's less than zero indicate unsatisfactory economics. Obviously if the NPV for the previous example were negative, the PVR would be negative, indicating unsatisfactory economics consistent with the NPV findings.

A project with a PVR greater than zero is _____ .
A project with a PVR equal to zero is _____ .
A project with a negative PVR is _____ .

Acceptable.
A breakeven with investing elsewhere at "i*".
Unacceptable.

10. In the preceding example there is only one cost, the initial expense of $20,000 at year 0. But we might have to contend with additional costs at various points in the project's life. When this occurs, this rule applies:

Only resultant costs that (after netting together the costs and incomes) are not offset by preceding income go into the denominator of the PVR fraction.

The following example illustrates the proper denominator for PVR calculations when more than one capital investment (or negative cash flow) is present in a project cash flow stream. The minimum rate of return is 15%.

$$\frac{\begin{matrix} & & \text{I=\$110} \\ \text{C=\$100} & \text{C=\$200} & \text{I=\$110 ......I=\$110} \end{matrix}}{\begin{matrix} 0 & 1 & 2............8 \end{matrix}} \quad \text{L=0}$$

To calculate the PVR numerator, we solve the following equation:

$$\text{NPV} = \$110(\overset{4.487}{P/A_{15\%,8}}) - \$200(\overset{.8696}{P/F_{15\%,1}}) - \$100 = +\$219.6$$

We now have the numerator (NPV), for the PVR fraction. Note that the $200 expense at the end of period one is discounted by i* for (how many) _____ periods?

─────────────────────

One Period. (See the single payment compound amount factor $(P/F_{15\%,1})$). If expenses had been incurred at other periods they would be accounted for in the same way.

11. To correctly compute the denominator we must first combine the revenue and capital investment cost in year one and discount the resulting "net amount" if that value is negative cash flow (a net cost). Therefore, the denominator for PVR calculations would appear as follows:

$$.8696$$
$$\text{PVR Denominator} = \$100 + \$90(P/F_{15\%,1}) = \$178.3$$

Given the NPV of +$219.6 and a denominator of $178.3, compute the project PVR and interpret the meaning of the result.

─────────────────────

PVR = $219.6/$178.3 = 1.23, > 0, Satisfactory investment. This +1.23 result represents dollars of NPV per present worth net equity cost dollar spent.

SKIP FRAME

If you feel confident with the previous calculations you may proceed to frame 23 and continue working ratio examples. Frames 12 through 22 present more detailed discussion of the proper determination of the PVR numerator and denominator.

12. Here is an example in which an operating cost occurs in more than one period where C = Capital Cost, OC = Operating Cost, L = Salvage:

		I=$150	I=$150	
C=$100	C=$90	OC=$40	OC=$40	L=$0
0	1	2 8		

The operating cost is $_____ and occurs in (how many) _____ periods?

─────────────────────

40, 7

13. In Frame 12, which costs should be included in the denominator of the PVR calculation?

———————————

The initial cost of $100 (at time zero), and the period 1 cost of $90. The year 2 through 8 costs are covered by project revenues in those years so do not affect the ratio denominator. This is the case whether costs are capital costs or operating costs.

14. Here is the numerator, or NPV equation for this problem:

NPV = $110(P/A_{15\%,7})(P/F_{15\%,1}) - 90(P/F_{15\%,1}) - 100$

What does the term $110(P/A_{15\%,7})(P/F_{15\%,1})$ do?

———————————

This term brings the seven uniform net revenues in years 2 through 8 back to the beginning of the first year for which there is a value, which is the end of year 1. This lump sum amount is then discounted one additional year (as a future sum) back to the present (time 0)

15. Note that the income and expenses for each of the 7 periods have been netted ($150 - $40 = $110) for use in the equation. Also, we see that the $90 expense at the end of period 1 is discounted one year and subtracted in computing NPV. Can you deduce why?

———————————

The $90 is a cost for a period with no income. It represents negative cash flow in year 1 and therefore must be discounted back one year to the present and subtracted from the discounted positive cash flows.

16. The initial capital cost of $100 is incurred at time zero. Why does it not require discounting?

———————————

It is already stated in present worth terms at the time we are calculating NPV.

17. Use the 15% tables or hand calculate the factors to compute the NPV for the Frame 12 project. The NPV for this project is _____. Now compare your answer to the one arrived at in Frame 10. The NPV's for these two projects are (equal/not equal) _____ .

219.6, equal

18. We have now developed and explained the numerator for the calculation of PVR in this example. In plain english, the denominator will be _____ . (See the solution to Frame 3 if you cannot answer this question.)

Present worth negative cash flow, or present worth of net costs not offset by revenue.

19. In this example, negative cash flow includes the time zero capital cost of _____ and the year one capital cost of _____ .

$100, $90

20. With which one of these costs is it necessary to account for the time value of money by discounting the cost at "i*"?

Year 1 Capital Cost of $90 must be discounted one year to year 0.

21. The denominator of the PVR fraction is computed as follows:

$100 + 90(P/F_{15\%,1}) = ?$

Use the appropriate table, or use the mathematical definition for the P/F factor, $(1/(1+i)^n)$, to complete the calculation.

$100 + 90(.8696) = 178.26$

22. Recalling that PVR is the ratio of NPV divided by the present worth negative cash flows, compute the project PVR.

$PVR = 219.6 / 178.26 = 1.23$

23. Now that we have defined PVR and how to properly calculate the ratio's numerator and denominator, we need to understand the applications that PVR is designed to help us with in economic evaluation work. The basic function of PVR is to serve as a tool for ranking projects when more than one project may be selected, (non-mutually exclusive alternative analysis). As we saw in the preceding module, Cumulative NPV may also be used to properly select more than one investment from a pool of available non-mutually exclusive alternatives.

    Properly ranking non-mutually exclusive alternatives with PVR will also result in selecting the projects that will maximize _____ _____ .

    Cumulative NPV.

24. If we are selecting only one of several alternatives, (mutually exclusive projects) the concept of incremental analysis must be introduced to the reader. This concept allows the evaluator to determine whether investments that are more capital intensive should be made if other less capital intensive alternatives are available. Incremental analysis means subtracting the less capital intensive alternative from the larger investment project. Incremental costs and revenues associated with the larger projects can then be evaluated to determine if the more capital intensive project is justified. If the incremental cash flow numbers generate acceptable NPV, ROR (see Module 5) or PVR, the project should be undertaken. Incremental analysis is required for proper NPV, ROR or PVR analysis

of all mutually exclusive alternatives. However incremental analysis always leads to selecting the alternative with maximum total investment NPV as emphasized earlier. Often this is not the alternative with the biggest PVR or ROR on total investment. The details of this concept are illustrated in the textbook but not in this manual.

No Response Required

25. PVR will consistently rank projects from which more than one project may be selected (non-mutually exclusive). Selecting the projects starting with the largest PVR in descending order will maximize cumulative NPV for a given budget.

   Therefore, use PVR to properly _____ independent alternative investments from which more than one may be chosen.

Rank

26. If we can only choose one alternative from several mutually exclusive choices, selecting the project with the largest PVR *is not always correct!* To properly evaluate mutually exclusive alternatives where only one investment opportunity may be selected you must make incremental present value ratio analysis to determine if sufficient incremental profits exist to cover the required additional investments and provide the acceptable minimum rate of return.

   If we have several ways of developing a property, from which only one may be chosen, _____ PVR analysis is required to make a proper economic evaluation.

incremental

27. The following examples illustrate the concepts of selecting the proper denominator in PVR calculations, ranking projects with PVR and select-

ing the proper project when only one project can be selected using incremental PVR analysis.

For purposes of this module, the student should concentrate on the concept of using PVR to properly rank alternatives, but recognize the economic limitation of this ratio for other uses previously mentioned.

28. Rank the following non-mutually exclusive alternatives "A" and "B" using PVR analysis for $i^* = 15\%$.

A)

	C=200		C=180	
C=100	I=110	I=110	I=110............I=110	
0	1	2	3.................8	

B)

	C=200		C=180		
C=100	I=110	I=0	I=220	I=110....I=110	
0	1	2	3	4........8	

━━━━━━━━━━━━━━━━━━━━━━━━━

A) PVR = 0.57
B) PVR = 0.51

If you had difficulty organizing the solution to this problem the correct solutions follow.

$$\text{NPV, A} = \overset{4.487}{110(P/A_{15,8})} - \overset{.6575}{180(P/F_{15,3})} - \overset{.8696}{200(P/F_{15,1})} - 100 = +101.3$$

$$\text{NPV, B} = (\overset{3.352}{110(P/A_{15,5})} + 40)(\overset{.6575}{P/F_{15,3}}) - \overset{.8696}{90(P/F_{15,1})} - 100 = +90.5$$

As an aside, since the NPV's for both projects are positive, we know the projects are economically acceptable and that the PVR will also be greater than zero and acceptable. Only when NPV is negative will the PVR also be negative, resulting in unfavorable economics.

The denominator in the PVR fraction uses net costs not covered by income from earlier years. The year 3 cost in project "B" is offset completely by project income in year 3 and the year 3 cost in project "A" is offset by project income in years 2 and 3. Therefore, the PVR's for these two projects are calculated as follows:

$$\text{PVR, A} = \frac{101.3}{100 + (200 - 110)(P/F_{15,1})} = 0.57$$

$$\text{PVR, B} = \frac{90.5}{100 + (200 - 110)(P/F_{15,1})} = 0.51$$

29. Determine the best economic way for a project development manager to allocate \$500,000 in the following independent projects if "i*" equals 20%.

A) $\dfrac{\text{C=\$200,000} \qquad \text{I=\$90,000}\ldots\ldots \text{I=\$90,000}}{0 \qquad\qquad\qquad 1 \ldots\ldots\ldots\ldots\ldots 6}$ L=0

B) $\dfrac{\text{C=\$500,000} \qquad \text{I=\$300,000}\ldots\ldots \text{I=\$300,000}}{0 \qquad\qquad\qquad 1 \ldots\ldots\ldots\ldots\ldots 3}$ L=0

C) $\dfrac{\text{C=\$300,000} \qquad \text{I=\$120,000}\ldots\ldots \text{I=\$120,000}}{0 \qquad\qquad\qquad 1 \ldots\ldots\ldots\ldots\ldots 5}$ L=\$100,000

$$\text{PVR, A} = \frac{\$90,000(P/A_{20,6}) - \$200,000}{\$200,000} = 0.50$$

$$\text{PVR, B} = \frac{\$300,000(P/A_{20,3}) - \$500,000}{\$500,000} = 0.26$$

$$\text{PVR, C} = \frac{\$120,000(P/A_{20,5}) + \$100,000(P/F_{20,5}) - \$300,000}{\$300,000} = 0.33$$

Ranking the independent projects in descending order of PVR we would select project "A" first, project "C" second, and project "B" third. For a budget of \$500,000 we would be limited to accepting only projects "A" and "C" for development, even though project "B" had acceptable economics.

30. Looking at the project NPV's may also help to solidify your understanding of PVR. This was not asked for in the problem statement in Frame 29 but is provided as a supplement for your understanding of the subject material.

Project A,	NPV = \$100,000	PVR = 0.50
Project B,	NPV = \$130,000	PVR = 0.26
Project C,	NPV = \$ 99,000	PVR = 0.33

Note that projects "A" and "C" give more cumulative NPV ($199,000) than project "B". However, if the problem statement had asked you to select a single project from the 3 mutually exclusive alternatives presented, which project would you have chosen? Why?

═══════════════════════════════════

Project "B", since we had $500,000 to invest and selecting this alternative would accrue the largest profit (NPV) for the company from investing in any of these individual projects and investing any extra budget dollars elsewhere at "i*" which gives zero NPV. Note that this is not the project with the largest PVR! Remember, when we can only select one project from a pool of available investments you must make incremental PVR analysis. The concept of proper incremental analysis will not be addressed in this manual.

31. Note that ranking investments with PVR results in selecting the projects that maximize cumulative NPV. Investing our $500,000 in projects "A" & "C" generates cumulative NPV of $199,000 which is greater than $130,000 from choosing project "B" alone.

═══════════════════════════════════

No Response Required

32. Remember that care must be exercised when costs and incomes occur together, as only resultant net costs (negative cash flow) not offset by previous positive cash flow are included in the denominator of the PVR fraction.

═══════════════════════════════════

No Response Required

33. Three unequal life non-mutually exclusive investment alternatives with costs, profits and salvage values as shown on the time diagrams are being considered. Select the independent projects that will maximize net worth for the company, given i* = 20%.

A) $\dfrac{\text{C=\$160,000} \quad \text{I=\$150,000} \ldots\ldots\ldots\ldots \text{I=\$150,000}}{0 \qquad\qquad\qquad 1\ldots\ldots\ldots\ldots\ldots\ldots\ldots\ldots 5}$ L=$50,000

B) $\dfrac{\text{C=\$320,000} \quad \text{I=\$275,000} \ldots\ldots\ldots \text{I=\$275,000}}{0 \qquad\qquad\qquad 1\ldots\ldots\ldots\ldots\ldots\ldots 4}$ L=$70,000

C) $\dfrac{\text{C=\$480,000} \quad \text{I=\$500,000} \ldots \text{I=\$500,000}}{0 \qquad\qquad\qquad 1\ldots\ldots\ldots\ldots 3}$ L=$100,000

PVR, A = 1.93,   PVR, B = 1.33,   PVR, C = 1.31

Select alternatives "A" and "B" as the most economic way to invest the $480,000 since they have the largest and next largest PVR values.

34. Processing equipment with an expected useful life of 4 years costs $10,000 new and is expected to have zero salvage value. Annual revenue each year of the life of this equipment is expected to be $12,000 and annual operating costs are expected to be $3,500. Calculate the PVR for this investment for i* = 15%.

$$\overset{2.855}{\text{PVR} = [(12{,}000\text{-}3{,}500)(P/A_{15,4}) - 10{,}000] / 10{,}000}$$

$$= 14{,}267 / 10{,}000 = +1.4267$$

35. Consider that a $1,000,000 cost was incurred at time 0 for research and development expenses. Revenue and operating costs per year are $800,000 and $200,000 respectively for years 1 to 10 assuming escalation of operating costs and sales revenue per year will offset each other allowing profits to remain constant over the next 10 years. Assume year 10 salvage value will be zero. Determine the project PVR for i* = 20%.

$$\overset{4.192}{\text{PVR} = [(800{,}000\text{-}200{,}000)(P/A_{20,10}) \text{-}1{,}000{,}000] /1{,}000{,}000}$$

$$= 1{,}515{,}200 / 1{,}000{,}000 = 1.5152$$

36. Present Value Ratio, Criterion Test

   1) Rank "A" and "B" as non-mutually exclusive alternatives using PVR analysis and a minimum rate of return of 20%.

   2) If only one of these projects could be selected because they are mutually exclusive, could we utilize the total investment PVR to evaluate these projects? If your answer is no, what evaluation technique would you recommend?

A)

	C=250	C=500 I=400 OC=100	I=400 OC=100	I=400 OC=100	I=400 OC=100	L=100
	0	1	2	3	4	

B)

	C=250	C=300	I=400 OC=50	I=400 OC=50	I=400 OC=50	L=50
	0	1	2	3	4	

===

Solution to Present Value Ratio, Criterion Test

Case 1.

$$\text{NPV, A} = (400\text{-}100)\overset{2.589}{(P/A_{20,4})} + 100\overset{.4823}{(P/F_{20,4})} - 500\overset{.8333}{(P/F_{20,1})} - 250$$

$$= +158.3$$

$$\text{NPV, B} = [(400\text{-}50)\overset{2.106}{(P/A_{20,3})} - 300]\overset{.8333}{(P/F_{20,1})} + 50\overset{.4823}{(P/F_{20,4})} - 250$$

$$= +138.35$$

$$\text{PVR, A} = 158.3 / [250 + 200\overset{.8333}{(P/F_{20,1})}] = 0.37993$$

$$\text{PVR, B} = 138.35 / [250 + 300(P/F_{20,1})] = 0.27671$$

Therefore, select project "A" first, followed by project "B". Both projects have acceptable economics.

Case 2.

NO. In order to make a valid economic evaluation of these alternatives when only one project may be selected, we must make *incremental PVR analysis.* *You cannot use total investment PVR* calculations to select the single mutually exclusive project that will maximize total profit to the company since the project with the largest PVR may not have the largest NPV. In this case it does, but often it does not.

MODULE 5

Rate of Return, ROR

1. In the preceding modules of this course we learned how to discount cash flows so they are stated in terms of present worth. The term "discount" implies a (reduction/increase) _____ in value.

Reduction.

2. In this module we will learn to use another valid *discounted cash flow* decision criterion called *Rate of Return*, or *(ROR)*.

The Rate of Return is that compound interest rate that when applied to project cash flow, discounts a project's positive cash flows to a value that exactly equals the project's discounted negative cash flows. In other words, ROR is the compound interest rate that makes net present value exactly equal to zero.

Another term that means the same thing as ROR (Rate of Return) is "Discounted Cash Flow Rate of Return", or DCFROR. In this self teaching manual we will use ROR; however, if you refer to the reference text and encounter DCFROR or ROR you will know that it means the same thing as _____ .

Rate of Return.

3. We said that ROR is the interest rate that makes a project's present worth positive cash flows exactly equal to its present worth negative cash flows. If we take the NPV equation:

NPV = Present Worth Positive Cash Flow @ i*
+ Present Worth Negative Cash Flow @ i*

Inserting the project ROR as the value of "i" to replace "i*", what will be the value of the project NPV?

Zero.

4. ROR has been defined as the "i" value that makes NPV equal to zero. You will remember this NPV equation;

$$NPV = I(P/A_{i,n}) + L(P/F_{i,n}) - C = 0$$

Where C = Cost, I = Income, L = Salvage Value and i = ROR

C	I	I
0	1..................... n	

Are both positive and negative cash flows considered in the equation? By which terms?

Yes. Income, I, and Salvage, L, are positive cash flow items. Cost, C, represents negative cash flow.

5. There are two reasons for calculating ROR. One is to determine the compound interest rate of return that will be received by investing in a particular project. The other is to determine the economic viability of the project by comparing the ROR to "i*", the minimum rate of return. The value of ROR must be found by trial and error calculations. All values in the net present value equation are known except for "i". One must solve these NPV equations using different values for "i" until the equation is satisfied.

Is it possible to explicitly solve a net present value type of equation for the value of "i"?

No, (except for some very simple situations). The value of "i" usually must be established by trial and error calculations.

6. To review, ROR is the compound interest rate of return that can be realized by investing in a project venture. It also is the discount rate that makes a project net present value (NPV) equal to zero. ROR is an economic decision criterion that, when properly applied, can be used to determine whether a project will be economically viable when compared with other available uses for the investment of capital, represented by "i*". You will remember that "i*" is the minimum rate of return that represents other opportunities for the investment of available capital. It also is referred to as the opportunity cost of capital or the compound interest rate that is foregone by not investing in alternative ventures. Projects with an ROR greater than the ROR on other opportunities for the investment of capital are considered acceptable.

Give two reasons for calculating ROR.

To determine the compound interest rate of return received by investing in a particular project, and to determine the economic viability of the investment by comparing ROR for the project with "i*".

7. As with all other economic decision criteria, including NPV and PVR, all cash flow amounts used in ROR calculations must be adjusted beforehand so that tax amounts reflect proper consideration of capital cost deductions such as depreciation, and amortization. The application of such considerations is beyond the scope of this module but it is assumed tax deductions are properly accounted for before we insert appropriate figures for taxes into all economic evaluations in this module.

How do we use ROR as an economic decision criterion?

We compare an ROR with "i*" to determine whether the project is economically viable.

8. In your own words, define rate of return, ROR.

━━━━━━━━━━━━━━━━━━━━━━━━━━━

The compound interest rate that makes NPV equal to zero.

9. We said that ROR is the discount rate that will set discounted positive cash flow exactly equal to discounted negative cash flow (or will set NPV exactly equal to zero). Now we need to understand the trial and error calculations that make up the interpolation process used to actually find the value of "i" that makes our NPV equation equal to zero.

As we do this we will determine the interest rates at which NPV changes sign, that is, it goes through zero and changes sign from positive to negative or vice versa.

Why will this tell us that we are close to the correct ROR value?

━━━━━━━━━━━━━━━━━━━━━━━━━━━

Because the correct value of ROR will set NPV exactly equal to zero, and in our calculations NPV will have passed through the zero point.

10. When we have determined the interest rates at which NPV changes sign (passes through zero) we can then calculate the ROR more accurately by linear interpolation.

Linear interpolation is the process of finding values between any two consecutive terms of a series assuming straight line variation of the values in between the known values.

If we had tables for all possible interest rates we could find the correct one. But because there are no tables in the reference text for, say, ROR = i = 16%, we must calculate the desired values by _____ , between ROR values of 15% and 20%.

━━━━━━━━━━━━━━━━━━━━━━━━━━━

interpolating.

11. We will now compute the project rate of return (ROR) for the following cash flows.

Annual Cash Flow	-10.0	4.0	4.5	5.0
Year	0	1	2	3

Present Worth Equation:

1) $0 = -10.0 + 4.0(P/F_{i,1}) + 4.5(P/F_{i,2}) + 5.0(P/F_{i,3})$

We must now find the interest rate that satisfies this equation, that is that makes the right side of the equation equal to the zero on the left. By trial and error we find that between interest rates of 15% and 20% the right side of our equation straddles zero as follows:

$i = 15\%: = -10.0 + 4.0(.8696) + 4.5(.7561) + 5.0(.6575) = +0.1683$

Since NPV is +0.1683 at a 15% interest rate, we know there is more than enough revenue to cover costs at a 15% ROR. Therefore the next trial should be at a higher interest rate, which is 20% in the tables available at the end of this manual.

$i = 20\%: = -10.0 + 4.0(.8333) + 4.5(.6944) + 5.0(.5787) = -0.6485$

No Response Required

12. We now know that the value of "i" (rate of return) that we are looking for to satisfy our present worth equation (NPV = 0) is somewhere between 15% and 20%. (Actually we can see by looking at the computed present values that it is much closer to 15% than 20%.)

Using interpolation techniques we can now calculate the project internal rate of return.

$$\text{Project ROR} = 15\% + \frac{(0.1683 - 0)(20\% - 15\%)}{(0.1683 - (-0.6485))} = 15\% + 1.0\%$$

$$= 16.0\%$$

Therefore, investing in this project will yield a compound interest rate, or rate of return of 16.0%. Is this project satisfactory compared to investing elsewhere at i* = 15% (yes/no) _____ .

Yes, ROR = 16.0% > i* = 15%

13. As was the case with present value ratio, when selecting only one project from several mutually exclusive alternatives, you *do not* always want to select the project with the largest ROR. To properly utilize ROR when selecting the best mutually exclusive project, *we must make incremental rate of return* calculations to determine if sufficient incremental revenues exist to cover incremental costs associated with more capital intensive alternatives.

Further, ROR is not a valid tool for ranking independent non-mutually exclusive alternatives from which more than one may be selected.

As was the case with the PVR module, the ROR module will concentrate on the concept of ROR. Application to specific evaluation situations and the meaning of these results are reserved for the textbook.

No Response Required

14. You now should be ready for a practice problem. If you have doubts about your ability to solve practice problems, you should re-read the material we have just discussed.

No Response Required

15. An investment of $1,000,000 made at time zero is to generate sales and operating costs per year of $800,000 and $600,000 respectively for years 1 to 10. Assume there is no escalation in operating costs or sales revenue and that the year 10 salvage value will be zero. Determine the project ROR.

Solution (in thousands of dollars):

Year	1 - 10
Sales	800
-Operating Costs	-600
Before-Tax Cash Flow	200

Placing this information on a time line diagram we have in thousands of dollars:

CF=-1,000   CF=200.......... CF=200   L=0

0   1 10

PW Equation: $0 = -1,000 + 200(P/A_{i,10})$

$1,000/200 = (P/A_{i,10}) = 5.000$

From the tables, or mathematically, we find:

$(P/A_{15\%,10}) = 5.019$
$(P/A_{20\%,10}) = 4.192$

We want the interest rate (ROR) that makes $P/A_{i,10} = 5.000$

By interpolation, we can calculate the project ROR.

$ROR = 15\% + 5\%[(5.019-5.000) / (5.019-4.912)] = 15.1\%$

16. A company invests $55 million in a project which will generate the following after-tax cash flows (in millions of dollars) for the next 10 years. Calculate the project ROR.

Cash Flow	-55	25	25	24.25	21.25	26.25
Year	0	1	2	3	4-9	10

Setting year 0 cost (which is negative cash flow) equal to present worth positive cash flow is equivalent to setting NPV = 0.

PW Eq: $55 = 25(P/A_{i,2}) + 24.25(P/F_{i,3}) + 21.25(P/A_{i,6})(P/F_{i,3})$

$+ 26.25(P/F_{i,10})$

In this equation we have left 55 on the left side of the equation, so we are interpolating around 55.

Try i $= 40\%$

$= 25(1.224) + 24.25(0.3644) + 21.25(2.168)(0.3644)$

$+ 26.25(0.0346)$

$= 57.1$

Try i $= 50\%$

$= 25(1.111) + 24.25(0.2963) + 21.25(1.824)(0.2963) +$

$26.25(.0173)$

$= 46.9$

We have 55 on the left side of our equation straddled between 57.1 and 46.9 on the right side.

By interpolation we can calculate the ROR:

ROR $= 40\% + 10\% [(57.1 - 55) / (57.1 - 46.9)]$

$= 42.06\%$

A programmed financial calculator gives an ROR of 41.80% for these cash flows. The programmed calculator interpolates over much smaller ROR increments so it effectively eliminates interpolation error. Our result of 42.06% is 0.26% high due to interpolation error. However, uncertainty associated with numbers that go into ROR analysis usually is far greater than interpolation error.

17. A mineral or petroleum reserve contains 500,000 tons of ore (or barrels of oil). It will be produced uniformly over the next 5 years, @ 100,000 tons or barrels per year. The ore (or oil) will be sold for $25 per ton (or barrel) in the first operating year, with price projected to escalate 5% annually thereafter. The mineral rights are to be acquired with a $1 million lease payment at time 0. Capital expenditures of $2.5 million are also incurred at time zero. Annual operating costs in year 1 are estimated to be $1 million, escalating by $150,000 annually for the remaining years. The property and equipment are expected to have no salvage value at the end of the project life. What before-tax ROR is the company receiving on its investment?

Cash Flow Calculations, (All Figures in $1,000)

Year	0	1	2	3	4	5
Revenue		2500	2625	2756	2894	3039
-Op. Cost		-1000	-1150	-1300	-1450	-1600
-Cap Costs	-2500					
-Lease	-1000					
Net CF	-3500	1500	1475	1456	1444	1439

Drawing a time line diagram we have:

Net CF	-3500	1500	1475	1456	1444	1439
Year	0	1	2	3	4	5

$$NPV = 0 = -3500 + 1500(P/F_{i,1}) + 1475(P/F_{i,2}) + 1456(P/F_{i,3})$$
$$+ 1444(P/F_{i,4}) + 1439(P/F_{i,5})$$

At i = 30%, PW Eq. = +82.498
At i = 40%, PW Eq. = -501.963

By interpolation we obtain:

ROR = 30% + 10%[(82.498 - 0) / (82.498 + 501.963)]

= 31.4%

18. As with all other decision criteria such as NPV and PVR, ROR calculations are very straight forward once the cash flows are determined.

The main disadvantage of the ROR method is that you cannot compare total investment results with other projects and determine which is the better "economic" alternative. This is due to the fact that ROR is a measure of the return received for a given level of investment. As an example, a project with a $10,000 investment yielding a 100% return would not provide a company with as much net profit as a mutually exclusive alternative project costing $50,000 and yielding a 50% internal rate of return. These two project ROR's cannot be compared, for valid economic decisions, you must make incremental analysis to determine if the additional $40,000 investment generates sufficient incremental positive cash flow to justify the added investment. This subject in addressed in detail in the reference textbook.

Several work exercises follow to assess your understanding of ROR calculations. Check your performance with the answers following each problem.

19. The following is the projected cash flow for an investment. What is the project ROR?

Year	0	1	2
Cash Flow	-100	50	70

12.32

$NPV = -100 + 50(P/F_{i,1}) + 70(P/F_{i,2})$

ROR = 12.4%, by trial and error between 12% and 15%

20. The following are cash flow estimates for a proposed project (figures in millions of dollars). Calculate the ROR for this new project. 23.6

If the company has an "i*" of 10%, would you recommend this project? yes

Year	0	1	2	3	4	5
Revenue				150	150	150
-Operating Costs				-75	-75	-75
-Capital Costs		-60	-60			
-Acquisition	-10					

Year	0	1	2	3	4	5
Revenue				150	150	150
-Operating Costs				-75	-75	-75
-Capital Costs		-60	-60			
-Acquisition	-10					
Net Cash Flow	-10	-60	-60	75	75	75

$NPV = 0 = -10 - 60(P/F_{i,1}) - 60(P/F_{i,2}) + 75(P/F_{i,3}) + 75(P/F_{i,4})$
$\qquad + 75(P/F_{i,5})$

or $\quad 0 = -10 - 60(P/A_{i,2}) + 75(P/A_{i,3})(P/F_{i,2})$

NPV @ i = 20% = +8.0

NPV @ i=25% = -2.7

$i = ROR = 20\% + 5\%[(8.0-0)/(8.0+2.7)] = 23.7\% > i* = 10\%$, so accept

21. If your answers are correct, you are ready for the ROR Criterion Test.

22. ROR Criterion Test.   25.6

Calculate the ROR for the following project estimated cash flows:

Cash Flow	-150	80	76	50	32
Year	0	1	2	3	4

Solution to ROR Criterion Test.

Cash Flow	-150	80	76	50	32
Year	0	1	2	3	4

PW Eq. $150 = 80(P/F_{i,1}) + 76(P/F_{i,2}) + 50(P/F_{i,3}) + 32(P/F_{i,4})$

For i = 25%, PW Eq = 151.3

For i = 30%, PW Eq = 140.5

By interpolation we can solve for the project ROR.

ROR $= 25\% + 5\%\,[(151.3\text{-}150) / (151.3\text{-}140.5)]$

$\quad = 25.6\%$

APPENDIX A: Discrete Interest, Discrete Value Factors

$$i = 0.50\%$$

n	$F/P_{i,n}$	$P/F_{i,n}$	$F/A_{i,n}$	$A/F_{i,n}$	$A/P_{i,n}$	$P/A_{i,n}$
1	1.0050	0.9950	1.0000	1.00000	1.00500	0.9950
2	1.0100	0.9901	2.0050	0.49875	0.50375	1.9851
3	1.0151	0.9851	3.0150	0.33167	0.33667	2.9702
4	1.0202	0.9802	4.0301	0.24813	0.25313	3.9505
5	1.0253	0.9754	5.0503	0.19801	0.20301	4.9259
6	1.0304	0.9705	6.0755	0.16460	0.16960	5.8964
7	1.0355	0.9657	7.1059	0.14073	0.14573	6.8621
8	1.0407	0.9609	8.1414	0.12283	0.12783	7.8230
9	1.0459	0.9561	9.1821	0.10891	0.11391	8.7791
10	1.0511	0.9513	10.2280	0.09777	0.10277	9.7304
11	1.0564	0.9466	11.2792	0.08866	0.09366	10.6770
12	1.0617	0.9419	12.3356	0.08107	0.08607	11.6189
13	1.0670	0.9372	13.3972	0.07464	0.07964	12.5562
14	1.0723	0.9326	14.4642	0.06914	0.07414	13.4887
15	1.0777	0.9279	15.5365	0.06436	0.06936	14.4166
16	1.0831	0.9233	16.6142	0.06019	0.06519	15.3399
17	1.0885	0.9187	17.6973	0.05651	0.06151	16.2586
18	1.0939	0.9141	18.7858	0.05323	0.05823	17.1728
19	1.0994	0.9096	19.8797	0.05030	0.05530	18.0824
20	1.1049	0.9051	20.9791	0.04767	0.05267	18.9874
21	1.1104	0.9006	22.0840	0.04528	0.05028	19.8880
22	1.1160	0.8961	23.1944	0.04311	0.04811	20.7841
23	1.1216	0.8916	24.3104	0.04113	0.04613	21.6757
24	1.1272	0.8872	25.4320	0.03932	0.04432	22.5629
25	1.1328	0.8828	26.5591	0.03765	0.04265	23.4456
26	1.1385	0.8784	27.6919	0.03611	0.04111	24.3240
27	1.1442	0.8740	28.8304	0.03469	0.03969	25.1980
28	1.1499	0.8697	29.9745	0.03336	0.03836	26.0677
29	1.1556	0.8653	31.1244	0.03213	0.03713	26.9330
30	1.1614	0.8610	32.2800	0.03098	0.03598	27.7941
35	1.1907	0.8398	38.1454	0.02622	0.03122	32.0354
36	1.1967	0.8356	39.3361	0.02542	0.03042	32.8710
40	1.2208	0.8191	44.1588	0.02265	0.02765	36.1722
45	1.2516	0.7990	50.3242	0.01987	0.02487	40.2072
50	1.2832	0.7793	56.6452	0.01765	0.02265	44.1428
55	1.3156	0.7601	63.1258	0.01584	0.02084	47.9814
60	1.3489	0.7414	69.7700	0.01433	0.01933	51.7256
65	1.3829	0.7231	76.5821	0.01306	0.01806	55.3775
70	1.4178	0.7053	83.5661	0.01197	0.01697	58.9394
75	1.4536	0.6879	90.7265	0.01102	0.01602	62.4136
80	1.4903	0.6710	98.0677	0.01020	0.01520	65.8023
85	1.5280	0.6545	105.5943	0.00947	0.01447	69.1075
90	1.5666	0.6383	113.3109	0.00883	0.01383	72.3313
95	1.6061	0.6226	121.2224	0.00825	0.01325	75.4757
100	1.6467	0.6073	129.3337	0.00773	0.01273	78.5426

$$i = 1.00\%$$

n	$F/P_{i,n}$	$P/F_{i,n}$	$F/A_{i,n}$	$A/F_{i,n}$	$A/P_{i,n}$	$P/A_{i,n}$
1	1.0100	0.9901	1.0000	1.00000	1.01000	0.9901
2	1.0201	0.9803	2.0100	0.49751	0.50751	1.9704
3	1.0303	0.9706	3.0301	0.33002	0.34002	2.9410
4	1.0406	0.9610	4.0604	0.24628	0.25628	3.9020
5	1.0510	0.9515	5.1010	0.19604	0.20604	4.8534
6	1.0615	0.9420	6.1520	0.16255	0.17255	5.7955
7	1.0721	0.9327	7.2135	0.13863	0.14863	6.7282
8	1.0829	0.9235	8.2857	0.12069	0.13069	7.6517
9	1.0937	0.9143	9.3685	0.10674	0.11674	8.5660
10	1.1046	0.9053	10.4622	0.09558	0.10558	9.4713
11	1.1157	0.8963	11.5668	0.08645	0.09645	10.3676
12	1.1268	0.8874	12.6825	0.07885	0.08885	11.2551
13	1.1381	0.8787	13.8093	0.07241	0.08241	12.1337
14	1.1495	0.8700	14.9474	0.06690	0.07690	13.0037
15	1.1610	0.8613	16.0969	0.06212	0.07212	13.8651
16	1.1726	0.8528	17.2579	0.05794	0.06794	14.7179
17	1.1843	0.8444	18.4304	0.05426	0.06426	15.5623
18	1.1961	0.8360	19.6147	0.05098	0.06098	16.3983
19	1.2081	0.8277	20.8109	0.04805	0.05805	17.2260
20	1.2202	0.8195	22.0190	0.04542	0.05542	18.0456
21	1.2324	0.8114	23.2392	0.04303	0.05303	18.8570
22	1.2447	0.8034	24.4716	0.04086	0.05086	19.6604
23	1.2572	0.7954	25.7163	0.03889	0.04889	20.4558
24	1.2697	0.7876	26.9735	0.03707	0.04707	21.2434
25	1.2824	0.7798	28.2432	0.03541	0.04541	22.0232
26	1.2953	0.7720	29.5256	0.03387	0.04387	22.7952
27	1.3082	0.7644	30.8209	0.03245	0.04245	23.5596
28	1.3213	0.7568	32.1291	0.03112	0.04112	24.3164
29	1.3345	0.7493	33.4504	0.02990	0.03990	25.0658
30	1.3478	0.7419	34.7849	0.02875	0.03875	25.8077
35	1.4166	0.7059	41.6603	0.02400	0.03400	29.4086
36	1.4308	0.6989	43.0769	0.02321	0.03321	30.1075
40	1.4889	0.6717	48.8864	0.02046	0.03046	32.8347
45	1.5648	0.6391	56.4811	0.01771	0.02771	36.0945
50	1.6446	0.6080	64.4632	0.01551	0.02551	39.1961
55	1.7285	0.5785	72.8525	0.01373	0.02373	42.1472
60	1.8167	0.5504	81.6697	0.01224	0.02224	44.9550
65	1.9094	0.5237	90.9366	0.01100	0.02100	47.6266
70	2.0068	0.4983	100.6763	0.00993	0.01993	50.1685
75	2.1091	0.4741	110.9128	0.00902	0.01902	52.5871
80	2.2167	0.4511	121.6715	0.00822	0.01822	54.8882
85	2.3298	0.4292	132.9790	0.00752	0.01752	57.0777
90	2.4486	0.4084	144.8633	0.00690	0.01690	59.1609
95	2.5735	0.3886	157.3538	0.00636	0.01636	61.1430
100	2.7048	0.3697	170.4814	0.00587	0.01587	63.0289

$i = 5.00\%$

n	$F/P_{i,n}$	$P/F_{i,n}$	$F/A_{i,n}$	$A/F_{i,n}$	$A/P_{i,n}$	$P/A_{i,n}$
1	1.0500	0.9524	1.0000	1.00000	1.05000	0.9524
2	1.1025	0.9070	2.0500	0.48780	0.53780	1.8594
3	1.1576	0.8638	3.1525	0.31721	0.36721	2.7232
4	1.2155	0.8227	4.3101	0.23201	0.28201	3.5460
5	1.2763	0.7835	5.5256	0.18097	0.23097	4.3295
6	1.3401	0.7462	6.8019	0.14702	0.19702	5.0757
7	1.4071	0.7107	8.1420	0.12282	0.17282	5.7864
8	1.4775	0.6768	9.5491	0.10472	0.15472	6.4632
9	1.5513	0.6446	11.0266	0.09069	0.14069	7.1078
10	1.6289	0.6139	12.5779	0.07950	0.12950	7.7217
11	1.7103	0.5847	14.2068	0.07039	0.12039	8.3064
12	1.7959	0.5568	15.9171	0.06283	0.11283	8.8633
13	1.8856	0.5303	17.7130	0.05646	0.10646	9.3936
14	1.9799	0.5051	19.5986	0.05102	0.10102	9.8986
15	2.0789	0.4810	21.5786	0.04634	0.09634	10.3797
16	2.1829	0.4581	23.6575	0.04227	0.09227	10.8378
17	2.2920	0.4363	25.8404	0.03870	0.08870	11.2741
18	2.4066	0.4155	28.1324	0.03555	0.08555	11.6896
19	2.5270	0.3957	30.5390	0.03275	0.08275	12.0853
20	2.6533	0.3769	33.0660	0.03024	0.08024	12.4622
21	2.7860	0.3589	35.7193	0.02800	0.07800	12.8212
22	2.9253	0.3418	38.5052	0.02597	0.07597	13.1630
23	3.0715	0.3256	41.4305	0.02414	0.07414	13.4886
24	3.2251	0.3101	44.5020	0.02247	0.07247	13.7986
25	3.3864	0.2953	47.7271	0.02095	0.07095	14.0939
26	3.5557	0.2812	51.1135	0.01956	0.06956	14.3752
27	3.7335	0.2678	54.6691	0.01829	0.06829	14.6430
28	3.9201	0.2551	58.4026	0.01712	0.06712	14.8981
29	4.1161	0.2429	62.3227	0.01605	0.06605	15.1411
30	4.3219	0.2314	66.4388	0.01505	0.06505	15.3725
31	4.5380	0.2204	70.7608	0.01413	0.06413	15.5928
32	4.7649	0.2099	75.2988	0.01328	0.06328	15.8027
33	5.0032	0.1999	80.0638	0.01249	0.06249	16.0025
34	5.2533	0.1904	85.0670	0.01176	0.06176	16.1929
35	5.5160	0.1813	90.3203	0.01107	0.06107	16.3742
36	5.7918	0.1727	95.8363	0.01043	0.06043	16.5469
37	6.0814	0.1644	101.6281	0.00984	0.05984	16.7113
38	6.3855	0.1566	107.7095	0.00928	0.05928	16.8679
39	6.7048	0.1491	114.0950	0.00876	0.05876	17.0170
40	7.0400	0.1420	120.7998	0.00828	0.05828	17.1591
48	10.4013	0.0961	188.0254	0.00532	0.05532	18.0772
50	11.4674	0.0872	209.3480	0.00478	0.05478	18.2559

i= 10.00%

n	$F/P_{i,n}$	$P/F_{i,n}$	$F/A_{i,n}$	$A/F_{i,n}$	$A/P_{i,n}$	$P/A_{i,n}$
1	1.1000	0.9091	1.0000	1.00000	1.10000	0.9091
2	1.2100	0.8264	2.1000	0.47619	0.57619	1.7355
3	1.3310	0.7513	3.3100	0.30211	0.40211	2.4869
4	1.4641	0.6830	4.6410	0.21547	0.31547	3.1699
5	1.6105	0.6209	6.1051	0.16380	0.26380	3.7908
6	1.7716	0.5645	7.7156	0.12961	0.22961	4.3553
7	1.9487	0.5132	9.4872	0.10541	0.20541	4.8684
8	2.1436	0.4665	11.4359	0.08744	0.18744	5.3349
9	2.3579	0.4241	13.5795	0.07364	0.17364	5.7590
10	2.5937	0.3855	15.9374	0.06275	0.16275	6.1446
11	2.8531	0.3505	18.5312	0.05396	0.15396	6.4951
12	3.1384	0.3186	21.3843	0.04676	0.14676	6.8137
13	3.4523	0.2897	24.5227	0.04078	0.14078	7.1034
14	3.7975	0.2633	27.9750	0.03575	0.13575	7.3667
15	4.1772	0.2394	31.7725	0.03147	0.13147	7.6061
16	4.5950	0.2176	35.9497	0.02782	0.12782	7.8237
17	5.0545	0.1978	40.5447	0.02466	0.12466	8.0216
18	5.5599	0.1799	45.5992	0.02193	0.12193	8.2014
19	6.1159	0.1635	51.1591	0.01955	0.11955	8.3649
20	6.7275	0.1486	57.2750	0.01746	0.11746	8.5136
21	7.4002	0.1351	64.0025	0.01562	0.11562	8.6487
22	8.1403	0.1228	71.4027	0.01401	0.11401	8.7715
23	8.9543	0.1117	79.5430	0.01257	0.11257	8.8832
24	9.8497	0.1015	88.4973	0.01130	0.11130	8.9847
25	10.8347	0.0923	98.3471	0.01017	0.11017	9.0770
26	11.9182	0.0839	109.1818	0.00916	0.10916	9.1609
27	13.1100	0.0763	121.0999	0.00826	0.10826	9.2372
28	14.4210	0.0693	134.2099	0.00745	0.10745	9.3066
29	15.8631	0.0630	148.6309	0.00673	0.10673	9.3696
30	17.4494	0.0573	164.4940	0.00608	0.10608	9.4269
31	19.1943	0.0521	181.9434	0.00550	0.10550	9.4790
32	21.1138	0.0474	201.1378	0.00497	0.10497	9.5264
33	23.2252	0.0431	222.2515	0.00450	0.10450	9.5694
34	25.5477	0.0391	245.4767	0.00407	0.10407	9.6086
35	28.1024	0.0356	271.0244	0.00369	0.10369	9.6442
36	30.9127	0.0323	299.1268	0.00334	0.10334	9.6765
37	34.0039	0.0294	330.0395	0.00303	0.10303	9.7059
38	37.4043	0.0267	364.0434	0.00275	0.10275	9.7327
39	41.1448	0.0243	401.4478	0.00249	0.10249	9.7570
40	45.2593	0.0221	442.5926	0.00226	0.10226	9.7791
48	97.0172	0.0103	960.1723	0.00104	0.10104	9.8969
50	117.3909	0.0085	1163.9085	0.00086	0.10086	9.9148

$$i = 12.00\%$$

n	$F/P_{i,n}$	$P/F_{i,n}$	$F/A_{i,n}$	$A/F_{i,n}$	$A/P_{i,n}$	$P/A_{i,n}$
1	1.1200	0.8929	1.0000	1.00000	1.12000	0.8929
2	1.2544	0.7972	2.1200	0.47170	0.59170	1.6901
3	1.4049	0.7118	3.3744	0.29635	0.41635	2.4018
4	1.5735	0.6355	4.7793	0.20923	0.32923	3.0373
5	1.7623	0.5674	6.3528	0.15741	0.27741	3.6048
6	1.9738	0.5066	8.1152	0.12323	0.24323	4.1114
7	2.2107	0.4523	10.0890	0.09912	0.21912	4.5638
8	2.4760	0.4039	12.2997	0.08130	0.20130	4.9676
9	2.7731	0.3606	14.7757	0.06768	0.18768	5.3282
10	3.1058	0.3220	17.5487	0.05698	0.17698	5.6502
11	3.4785	0.2875	20.6546	0.04842	0.16842	5.9377
12	3.8960	0.2567	24.1331	0.04144	0.16144	6.1944
13	4.3635	0.2292	28.0291	0.03568	0.15568	6.4235
14	4.8871	0.2046	32.3926	0.03087	0.15087	6.6282
15	5.4736	0.1827	37.2797	0.02682	0.14682	6.8109
16	6.1304	0.1631	42.7533	0.02339	0.14339	6.9740
17	6.8660	0.1456	48.8837	0.02046	0.14046	7.1196
18	7.6900	0.1300	55.7497	0.01794	0.13794	7.2497
19	8.6128	0.1161	63.4397	0.01576	0.13576	7.3658
20	9.6463	0.1037	72.0524	0.01388	0.13388	7.4694
21	10.8038	0.0926	81.6987	0.01224	0.13224	7.5620
22	12.1003	0.0826	92.5026	0.01081	0.13081	7.6446
23	13.5523	0.0738	104.6029	0.00956	0.12956	7.7184
24	15.1786	0.0659	118.1552	0.00846	0.12846	7.7843
25	17.0001	0.0588	133.3339	0.00750	0.12750	7.8431
26	19.0401	0.0525	150.3339	0.00665	0.12665	7.8957
27	21.3249	0.0469	169.3740	0.00590	0.12590	7.9426
28	23.8839	0.0419	190.6989	0.00524	0.12524	7.9844
29	26.7499	0.0374	214.5828	0.00466	0.12466	8.0218
30	29.9599	0.0334	241.3327	0.00414	0.12414	8.0552
31	33.5551	0.0298	271.2926	0.00369	0.12369	8.0850
32	37.5817	0.0266	304.8477	0.00328	0.12328	8.1116
33	42.0915	0.0238	342.4294	0.00292	0.12292	8.1354
34	47.1425	0.0212	384.5210	0.00260	0.12260	8.1566
35	52.7996	0.0189	431.6635	0.00232	0.12232	8.1755
36	59.1356	0.0169	484.4631	0.00206	0.12206	8.1924
37	66.2318	0.0151	543.5987	0.00184	0.12184	8.2075
38	74.1797	0.0135	609.8305	0.00164	0.12164	8.2210
39	83.0812	0.0120	684.0102	0.00146	0.12146	8.2330
40	93.0510	0.0107	767.0914	0.00130	0.12130	8.2438
48	230.3908	0.0043	1911.5898	0.00052	0.12052	8.2972
50	289.0022	0.0035	2400.0182	0.00042	0.12042	8.3045

$$i = 15.00\%$$

n	$F/P_{i,n}$	$P/F_{i,n}$	$F/A_{i,n}$	$A/F_{i,n}$	$A/P_{i,n}$	$P/A_{i,n}$
1	1.1500	0.8696	1.0000	1.00000	1.15000	0.8696
2	1.3225	0.7561	2.1500	0.46512	0.61512	1.6257
3	1.5209	0.6575	3.4725	0.28798	0.43798	2.2832
4	1.7490	0.5718	4.9934	0.20027	0.35027	2.8550
5	2.0114	0.4972	6.7424	0.14832	0.29832	3.3522
6	2.3131	0.4323	8.7537	0.11424	0.26424	3.7845
7	2.6600	0.3759	11.0668	0.09036	0.24036	4.1604
8	3.0590	0.3269	13.7268	0.07285	0.22285	4.4873
9	3.5179	0.2843	16.7858	0.05957	0.20957	4.7716
10	4.0456	0.2472	20.3037	0.04925	0.19925	5.0188
11	4.6524	0.2149	24.3493	0.04107	0.19107	5.2337
12	5.3503	0.1869	29.0017	0.03448	0.18448	5.4206
13	6.1528	0.1625	34.3519	0.02911	0.17911	5.5831
14	7.0757	0.1413	40.5047	0.02469	0.17469	5.7245
15	8.1371	0.1229	47.5804	0.02102	0.17102	5.8474
16	9.3576	0.1069	55.7175	0.01795	0.16795	5.9542
17	10.7613	0.0929	65.0751	0.01537	0.16537	6.0472
18	12.3755	0.0808	75.8364	0.01319	0.16319	6.1280
19	14.2318	0.0703	88.2118	0.01134	0.16134	6.1982
20	16.3665	0.0611	102.4436	0.00976	0.15976	6.2593
21	18.8215	0.0531	118.8101	0.00842	0.15842	6.3125
22	21.6447	0.0462	137.6316	0.00727	0.15727	6.3587
23	24.8915	0.0402	159.2764	0.00628	0.15628	6.3988
24	28.6252	0.0349	184.1678	0.00543	0.15543	6.4338
25	32.9190	0.0304	212.7930	0.00470	0.15470	6.4641
26	37.8568	0.0264	245.7120	0.00407	0.15407	6.4906
27	43.5353	0.0230	283.5688	0.00353	0.15353	6.5135
28	50.0656	0.0200	327.1041	0.00306	0.15306	6.5335
29	57.5755	0.0174	377.1697	0.00265	0.15265	6.5509
30	66.2118	0.0151	434.7451	0.00230	0.15230	6.5660
31	76.1435	0.0131	500.9569	0.00200	0.15200	6.5791
32	87.5651	0.0114	577.1005	0.00173	0.15173	6.5905
33	100.6998	0.0099	664.6655	0.00150	0.15150	6.6005
34	115.8048	0.0086	765.3654	0.00131	0.15131	6.6091
35	133.1755	0.0075	881.1702	0.00113	0.15113	6.6166
36	153.1519	0.0065	1014.3457	0.00099	0.15099	6.6231
37	176.1246	0.0057	1167.4975	0.00086	0.15086	6.6288
38	202.5433	0.0049	1343.6222	0.00074	0.15074	6.6338
39	232.9248	0.0043	1546.1655	0.00065	0.15065	6.6380
40	267.8635	0.0037	1779.0903	0.00056	0.15056	6.6418
48	819.4007	0.0012	5456.0047	0.00018	0.15018	6.6585
50	1083.6574	0.0009	7217.7163	0.00014	0.15014	6.6605

i = 20.00%

n	F/P$_{i,n}$	P/F$_{i,n}$	F/A$_{i,n}$	A/F$_{i,n}$	A/P$_{i,n}$	P/A$_{i,n}$
1	1.2000	0.8333	1.0000	1.00000	1.20000	0.8333
2	1.4400	0.6944	2.2000	0.45455	0.65455	1.5278
3	1.7280	0.5787	3.6400	0.27473	0.47473	2.1065
4	2.0736	0.4823	5.3680	0.18629	0.38629	2.5887
5	2.4883	0.4019	7.4416	0.13438	0.33438	2.9906
6	2.9860	0.3349	9.9299	0.10071	0.30071	3.3255
7	3.5832	0.2791	12.9159	0.07742	0.27742	3.6046
8	4.2998	0.2326	16.4991	0.06061	0.26061	3.8372
9	5.1598	0.1938	20.7989	0.04808	0.24808	4.0310
10	6.1917	0.1615	25.9587	0.03852	0.23852	4.1925
11	7.4301	0.1346	32.1504	0.03110	0.23110	4.3271
12	8.9161	0.1122	39.5805	0.02526	0.22526	4.4392
13	10.6993	0.0935	48.4966	0.02062	0.22062	4.5327
14	12.8392	0.0779	59.1959	0.01689	0.21689	4.6106
15	15.4070	0.0649	72.0351	0.01388	0.21388	4.6755
16	18.4884	0.0541	87.4421	0.01144	0.21144	4.7296
17	22.1861	0.0451	105.9306	0.00944	0.20944	4.7746
18	26.6233	0.0376	128.1167	0.00781	0.20781	4.8122
19	31.9480	0.0313	154.7400	0.00646	0.20646	4.8435
20	38.3376	0.0261	186.6880	0.00536	0.20536	4.8696
21	46.0051	0.0217	225.0256	0.00444	0.20444	4.8913
22	55.2061	0.0181	271.0307	0.00369	0.20369	4.9094
23	66.2474	0.0151	326.2369	0.00307	0.20307	4.9245
24	79.4968	0.0126	392.4842	0.00255	0.20255	4.9371
25	95.3962	0.0105	471.9811	0.00212	0.20212	4.9476
26	114.4755	0.0087	567.3773	0.00176	0.20176	4.9563
27	137.3706	0.0073	681.8528	0.00147	0.20147	4.9636
28	164.8447	0.0061	819.2233	0.00122	0.20122	4.9697
29	197.8136	0.0051	984.0680	0.00102	0.20102	4.9747
30	237.3763	0.0042	1181.8816	0.00085	0.20085	4.9789
31	284.8516	0.0035	1419.2579	0.00070	0.20070	4.9824
32	341.8219	0.0029	1704.1095	0.00059	0.20059	4.9854
33	410.1863	0.0024	2045.9314	0.00049	0.20049	4.9878
34	492.2235	0.0020	2456.1176	0.00041	0.20041	4.9898
35	590.6682	0.0017	2948.3411	0.00034	0.20034	4.9915
36	708.8019	0.0014	3539.0094	0.00028	0.20028	4.9929
37	850.5622	0.0012	4247.8112	0.00024	0.20024	4.9941
38	1020.6747	0.0010	5098.3735	0.00020	0.20020	4.9951
39	1224.8096	0.0008	6119.0482	0.00016	0.20016	4.9959
40	1469.7716	0.0007	7343.8578	0.00014	0.20014	4.9966
48	6319.7487	0.0002	31593.7436	0.00003	0.20003	4.9992
50	9100.4382	0.0001	45497.1908	0.00002	0.20002	4.9995

$$i = 25.00\%$$

n	$F/P_{i,n}$	$P/F_{i,n}$	$F/A_{i,n}$	$A/F_{i,n}$	$A/P_{i,n}$	$P/A_{i,n}$
1	1.2500	0.8000	1.0000	1.00000	1.25000	0.8000
2	1.5625	0.6400	2.2500	0.44444	0.69444	1.4400
3	1.9531	0.5120	3.8125	0.26230	0.51230	1.9520
4	2.4414	0.4096	5.7656	0.17344	0.42344	2.3616
5	3.0518	0.3277	8.2070	0.12185	0.37185	2.6893
6	3.8147	0.2621	11.2588	0.08882	0.33882	2.9514
7	4.7684	0.2097	15.0735	0.06634	0.31634	3.1611
8	5.9605	0.1678	19.8419	0.05040	0.30040	3.3289
9	7.4506	0.1342	25.8023	0.03876	0.28876	3.4631
10	9.3132	0.1074	33.2529	0.03007	0.28007	3.5705
11	11.6415	0.0859	42.5661	0.02349	0.27349	3.6564
12	14.5519	0.0687	54.2077	0.01845	0.26845	3.7251
13	18.1899	0.0550	68.7596	0.01454	0.26454	3.7801
14	22.7374	0.0440	86.9495	0.01150	0.26150	3.8241
15	28.4217	0.0352	109.6868	0.00912	0.25912	3.8593
16	35.5271	0.0281	138.1085	0.00724	0.25724	3.8874
17	44.4089	0.0225	173.6357	0.00576	0.25576	3.9099
18	55.5112	0.0180	218.0446	0.00459	0.25459	3.9279
19	69.3889	0.0144	273.5558	0.00366	0.25366	3.9424
20	86.7362	0.0115	342.9447	0.00292	0.25292	3.9539
21	108.4202	0.0092	429.6809	0.00233	0.25233	3.9631
22	135.5253	0.0074	538.1011	0.00186	0.25186	3.9705
23	169.4066	0.0059	673.6264	0.00148	0.25148	3.9764
24	211.7582	0.0047	843.0329	0.00119	0.25119	3.9811
25	264.6978	0.0038	1054.7912	0.00095	0.25095	3.9849
26	330.8722	0.0030	1319.4890	0.00076	0.25076	3.9879
27	413.5903	0.0024	1650.3612	0.00061	0.25061	3.9903
28	516.9879	0.0019	2063.9515	0.00048	0.25048	3.9923
29	646.2349	0.0015	2580.9394	0.00039	0.25039	3.9938
30	807.7936	0.0012	3227.1743	0.00031	0.25031	3.9950
31	1009.7420	0.0010	4034.9678	0.00025	0.25025	3.9960
32	1262.1774	0.0008	5044.7098	0.00020	0.25020	3.9968
33	1577.7218	0.0006	6306.8872	0.00016	0.25016	3.9975
34	1972.1523	0.0005	7884.6091	0.00013	0.25013	3.9980
35	2465.1903	0.0004	9856.7613	0.00010	0.25010	3.9984
36	3081.4879	0.0003	12321.9516	0.00008	0.25008	3.9987
37	3851.8599	0.0003	15403.4396	0.00006	0.25006	3.9990
38	4814.8249	0.0002	19255.2994	0.00005	0.25005	3.9992
39	6018.5311	0.0002	24070.1243	0.00004	0.25004	3.9993
40	7523.1638	0.0001	30088.6554	0.00003	0.25003	3.9995

$$i = 30.00\%$$

n	$F/P_{i,n}$	$P/F_{i,n}$	$F/A_{i,n}$	$A/F_{i,n}$	$A/P_{i,n}$	$P/A_{i,n}$
1	1.3000	0.7692	1.0000	1.00000	1.30000	0.7692
2	1.6900	0.5917	2.3000	0.43478	0.73478	1.3609
3	2.1970	0.4552	3.9900	0.25063	0.55063	1.8161
4	2.8561	0.3501	6.1870	0.16163	0.46163	2.1662
5	3.7129	0.2693	9.0431	0.11058	0.41058	2.4356
6	4.8268	0.2072	12.7560	0.07839	0.37839	2.6427
7	6.2749	0.1594	17.5828	0.05687	0.35687	2.8021
8	8.1573	0.1226	23.8577	0.04192	0.34192	2.9247
9	10.6045	0.0943	32.0150	0.03124	0.33124	3.0190
10	13.7858	0.0725	42.6195	0.02346	0.32346	3.0915
11	17.9216	0.0558	56.4053	0.01773	0.31773	3.1473
12	23.2981	0.0429	74.3270	0.01345	0.31345	3.1903
13	30.2875	0.0330	97.6250	0.01024	0.31024	3.2233
14	39.3738	0.0254	127.9125	0.00782	0.30782	3.2487
15	51.1859	0.0195	167.2863	0.00598	0.30598	3.2682
16	66.5417	0.0150	218.4722	0.00458	0.30458	3.2832
17	86.5042	0.0116	285.0139	0.00351	0.30351	3.2948
18	112.4554	0.0089	371.5180	0.00269	0.30269	3.3037
19	146.1920	0.0068	483.9734	0.00207	0.30207	3.3105
20	190.0496	0.0053	630.1655	0.00159	0.30159	3.3158
21	247.0645	0.0040	820.2151	0.00122	0.30122	3.3198
22	321.1839	0.0031	1067.2796	0.00094	0.30094	3.3230
23	417.5391	0.0024	1388.4635	0.00072	0.30072	3.3254
24	542.8008	0.0018	1806.0026	0.00055	0.30055	3.3272
25	705.6410	0.0014	2348.8033	0.00043	0.30043	3.3286
26	917.3333	0.0011	3054.4443	0.00033	0.30033	3.3297
27	1192.5333	0.0008	3971.7776	0.00025	0.30025	3.3305
28	1550.2933	0.0006	5164.3109	0.00019	0.30019	3.3312
29	2015.3813	0.0005	6714.6042	0.00015	0.30015	3.3317
30	2619.9956	0.0004	8729.9855	0.00011	0.30011	3.3321
31	3405.9943	0.0003	11349.9811	0.00009	0.30009	3.3324
32	4427.7926	0.0002	14755.9755	0.00007	0.30007	3.3326
33	5756.1304	0.0002	19183.7681	0.00005	0.30005	3.3328
34	7482.9696	0.0001	24939.8985	0.00004	0.30004	3.3329
35	9727.8604	0.0001	32422.8681	0.00003	0.30003	3.3330

i = 40.00%

n	$F/P_{i,n}$	$P/F_{i,n}$	$F/A_{i,n}$	$A/F_{i,n}$	$A/P_{i,n}$	$P/A_{i,n}$
1	1.4000	0.7143	1.0000	1.00000	1.40000	0.7143
2	1.9600	0.5102	2.4000	0.41667	0.81667	1.2245
3	2.7440	0.3644	4.3600	0.22936	0.62936	1.5889
4	3.8416	0.2603	7.1040	0.14077	0.54077	1.8492
5	5.3782	0.1859	10.9456	0.09136	0.49136	2.0352
6	7.5295	0.1328	16.3238	0.06126	0.46126	2.1680
7	10.5414	0.0949	23.8534	0.04192	0.44192	2.2628
8	14.7579	0.0678	34.3947	0.02907	0.42907	2.3306
9	20.6610	0.0484	49.1526	0.02034	0.42034	2.3790
10	28.9255	0.0346	69.8137	0.01432	0.41432	2.4136
11	40.4957	0.0247	98.7391	0.01013	0.41013	2.4383
12	56.6939	0.0176	139.2348	0.00718	0.40718	2.4559
13	79.3715	0.0126	195.9287	0.00510	0.40510	2.4685
14	111.1201	0.0090	275.3002	0.00363	0.40363	2.4775
15	155.5681	0.0064	386.4202	0.00259	0.40259	2.4839
16	217.7953	0.0046	541.9883	0.00185	0.40185	2.4885
17	304.9135	0.0033	759.7837	0.00132	0.40132	2.4918
18	426.8789	0.0023	1064.6971	0.00094	0.40094	2.4941
19	597.6304	0.0017	1491.5760	0.00067	0.40067	2.4958
20	836.6826	0.0012	2089.2064	0.00048	0.40048	2.4970
21	1171.3556	0.0009	2925.8889	0.00034	0.40034	2.4979
22	1639.8978	0.0006	4097.2445	0.00024	0.40024	2.4985
23	2295.8569	0.0004	5737.1423	0.00017	0.40017	2.4989
24	3214.1997	0.0003	8032.9993	0.00012	0.40012	2.4992
25	4499.8796	0.0002	11247.1990	0.00009	0.40009	2.4994
26	6299.8314	0.0002	15747.0785	0.00006	0.40006	2.4996
27	8819.7640	0.0001	22046.9099	0.00005	0.40005	2.4997
28	12347.6696	0.0001	30866.6739	0.00003	0.40003	2.4998
29	17286.7374	0.0001	43214.3435	0.00002	0.40002	2.4999
30	24201.4324	0.0000	60501.0809	0.00002	0.40002	2.4999

$$i = 50.00\%$$

n	$F/P_{i,n}$	$P/F_{i,n}$	$F/A_{i,n}$	$A/F_{i,n}$	$A/P_{i,n}$	$P/A_{i,n}$
1	1.5000	0.6667	1.0000	1.00000	1.50000	0.6667
2	2.2500	0.4444	2.5000	0.40000	0.90000	1.1111
3	3.3750	0.2963	4.7500	0.21053	0.71053	1.4074
4	5.0625	0.1975	8.1250	0.12308	0.62308	1.6049
5	7.5938	0.1317	13.1875	0.07583	0.57583	1.7366
6	11.3906	0.0878	20.7813	0.04812	0.54812	1.8244
7	17.0859	0.0585	32.1719	0.03108	0.53108	1.8829
8	25.6289	0.0390	49.2578	0.02030	0.52030	1.9220
9	38.4434	0.0260	74.8867	0.01335	0.51335	1.9480
10	57.6650	0.0173	113.3301	0.00882	0.50882	1.9653
11	86.4976	0.0116	170.9951	0.00585	0.50585	1.9769
12	129.7463	0.0077	257.4927	0.00388	0.50388	1.9846
13	194.6195	0.0051	387.2390	0.00258	0.50258	1.9897
14	291.9293	0.0034	581.8585	0.00172	0.50172	1.9931
15	437.8939	0.0023	873.7878	0.00114	0.50114	1.9954
16	656.8408	0.0015	1311.6817	0.00076	0.50076	1.9970
17	985.2613	0.0010	1968.5225	0.00051	0.50051	1.9980
18	1477.8919	0.0007	2953.7838	0.00034	0.50034	1.9986
19	2216.8378	0.0005	4431.6756	0.00023	0.50023	1.9991
20	3325.2567	0.0003	6648.5135	0.00015	0.50015	1.9994
21	4987.8851	0.0002	9973.7702	0.00010	0.50010	1.9996
22	7481.8276	0.0001	14961.6553	0.00007	0.50007	1.9997
23	11222.7415	0.0001	22443.4829	0.00004	0.50004	1.9998
24	16834.1122	0.0001	33666.2244	0.00003	0.50003	1.9999
25	25251.1683	0.0000	50500.3366	0.00002	0.50002	1.9999
26	37876.7524	0.0000	75751.5049	0.00001	0.50001	1.9999
27	56815.1287	0.0000	113628.2573	0.00001	0.50001	2.0000
28	85222.6930	0.0000	170443.3860	0.00001	0.50001	2.0000
29	127834.0395	0.0000	255666.0790	0.00000	0.50000	2.0000
30	191751.0592	0.0000	383500.1185	0.00000	0.50000	2.0000